W9-CPR-081

ainsley
harriott's
low-fat
meals
in minutes

ainsley harriott's low-fat meals in minutes

Acknowledgments

Thank you so much to Lorna Brash for all her hard work
and for testing all the recipes. Also to Howard Shooter
for the superb food photography. Thanks to all at
BBC Books, especially my commissioning editor Nicky
Copeland, project editor Rachel Copus and designers
Sarah Ponder and Susannah Good. Thanks also to my
agents Jerry 'Zola' Hicks, Sarah and Julie Dalkin and, of
course, to my understanding wife Clare and our special
kids Jimmy and Madeleine. And finally to Oscar the dog –
more walks on the way, boy.

LONDON, NEW YORK, MUNICH,
MELBOURNE, and DELHI
Project Editor: Barbara Berger
Creative Director: Tina Vaughan
Project Director: Valerie Buckingham
Publisher: Chuck Lang
Production Manager: Chris Avgherinos
DTP Designer: Milos Orlovic
Copy Editor: Laaren Brown
Editorial Assistant: Madeline Farber

First American Edition, 2002
00 01 02 03 04 05 10 9 8 7 6 5 4 3 2 1
Published in the United States
by DK Publishing, Inc.
375 Hudson Street
New York, New York 10014

Ainsley Harriot's Low-Fat Meals in Minutes
ISBN 0-7894-9302-2

Cataloguing in Publication data is available from the
Library of Congress

Published by BBC Worldwide Limited,
Woodlands, 80 Wood Lane, London W12 0TT
First published 2002
Text © Ainsley Harriott 2002
The moral right of the author has been asserted

All food photography by Howard Shooter (assistant
Mike Hart) except the following: 24, 29, 33, 40, 49, 56,
64, 74, 110, 115, 143, 182 and 189 (Gus Filgate); 59,
170 (Juliet Piddington) all © BBC Worldwide; 181, 185
(Roger Stowell) © Roger Stowell
Jacket and location photography by Craig Easton © BBC
Worldwide 2002

Recipes developed and written in association with
Lorna Brash

Commissioning Editor: Nicky Copeland
Project Editor: Rachel Copus
Cover Art Director: Pene Parker
Book Art Director: Sarah Ponder
Designer: Susannah Good
Production Controller: Kenneth McKay
Food Stylist: Lorna Brash
Props Stylist: Marian Price

Set in Humanist
Printed and bound in Italy by LEGO Spa
Color separations by Kestrel Digital Colour, Chelmsford

All the spoon measurements in this book are level unless
otherwise stated. A tablespoon is 15 ml; a teaspoon is
5 ml. Follow one set of measurements when preparing
any of the recipes. Do not mix metric with imperial. All
eggs used in the recipes are medium sized. All vegetables
should be peeled unless the recipe says otherwise.

Contents

Introduction

I want this book to be all about enjoying food, reducing fat but still offering quick, tasty, and substantial meals that are more of a healthy eating celebration than a punishment. Let's face it, there's no point in serving up smaller portions on smaller plates to make them look bigger, or dishing up something bland and uninteresting. It's more a case of creating a healthier lifestyle—and even more importantly, fitting that lifestyle in and around our work and families. This will inevitably bring about some changes in the kitchen, but it doesn't mean you have to lose out on taste.

There is an increasing emphasis on health-related matters, in magazines, books and on television—even on *Ready Steady Cook* we try to accommodate all types of diet, whether it's gluten-free, reduced sugar, or low fat. *Low-Fat Meals in Minutes* contains a mouth-watering collection of recipes that are packed full of flavor and draw on the fantastic range of fresh produce available in our supermarkets. I've combined classic ingredients with more recent arrivals in our shops—you'll be amazed at the wonderful selection of dishes you can throw together in the kitchen. And they're all totally satisfying.

From soups, starters, and snacks through to fish, chicken, meat and vegetarian dishes and finishing with low-fat desserts, there is something to appeal to everyone. Choose from Roasted Tomato, Thyme, and Crème Fraîche Soup (page 28), Classic Moules Marinière (page 58), Harissa Lamb with Low-Fat Hummus (page 114) and, for dessert, my Iced Passion-Fruit Platter (page 172).

With 80 recipes and a color photograph to accompany each one, you'll have a hard time choosing. Happy low-fat cooking! See you next time, healthier than ever and ready for more!

Fat facts

If you enjoy cooking and eating food as much as I do, it can be very easy to pile on the pounds. While many people panic and embark on drastic diets, it's much more effective to look at what we eat and try to make some changes. Cutting back on fat is the best place to start – and it doesn't have to be a hardship.

Why low fat?

I love food, and I really enjoy a bit of butter on my baked potato or a dollop of whipped cream on my dessert, so I bet you're wondering why I'm rattling on about cutting back on fat. Well, the fact is that while we all need a certain amount of fat to survive, too much of it can lead to all sorts of nasties, like heart disease and obesity, so it's in our interests to cut back. But don't feel that you're going to have to miss out. The point of this book is to show you how to cut out the fat . . . and still live life to the fullest.

Good fats and bad fats

Think of fat as an energy source. The fat that we take into our body in the form of food is broken down into units of energy that the body uses as fuel. We need to eat enough of it to give us the energy we need, but not too much. Fats are made up of fatty acids and can be divided into two main types: saturated and unsaturated.

Saturated fats are not essential to the body, so it's these fats that we should cut back on. Everyone knows to go easy on cream and butter, but saturated fats also lurk in full-fat dairy products such as cheese, whole milk—even cottage cheese—and are hidden in cakes, cookies, store-bought pies, and candy. Unsaturated fats are split into two groups, polyunsaturated and monounsaturated, both of which are important as part of a well-balanced diet. These exist in vegetable oils, oily fish (such as salmon, tuna, and mackerel), olive oil, canola oil, seeds, and nuts.

How much fat is too much?

The most recent recommendations from the Department of Health and Human Services show that in the United States we do need to reduce our fat intake. Our consumption of fat should be about 30% of our total calorie intake; at the moment it accounts for about 34%. As a rough guide, women should take in about 2,000 calories each day, about 600 from fat—that is approximately 65 g of fat. Active men should take in about 2,800 calories each day, 93 g of which may come from fat. I've used this as a guideline when choosing the recipes for this book and none of them contain more than 12 g of fat per serving. We should also watch our intake of saturated fat; it raises cholesterol more than other kinds of fat. (In a 2,000-calorie diet, 20 g of saturated fat is the Daily Value on product Nutrition Facts.) Saturated fat comes mostly from animal sources—meat and dairy products. One easy way to cut back on fat and saturated fat is to cut back on meat. Although it's full of protein, meat is quite high in fat, so try not to eat it for every meal. Why not give some of my vegetarian dishes a try? They really are delicious.

In the know

You can begin your new low-fat style of eating by experimenting with my recipes, but you can give your new regimen an even bigger kick start by choosing lower-fat versions of the dairy products in your diet. I've included a table, right, of some common foods and their low-fat equivalents. Take a look at the difference in fat content. You'll be inspired.

How to use this book
You really don't need to starve yourself, even if you are cutting down on your fat intake, so my main-course recipes include suggestions for side dishes. If the accompaniment is part of the recipe, for example, the burger bun in my Spicy Beanburger recipe (page 126), then the nutritional information for it is included in the overall analysis. However, if the recipe states "served with plain boiled rice," for example, you will need to allow for the extra fat included in the accompaniment, as shown on the chart, below.

Don't forget that you can mix and match from the side dishes. Each quantity is enough for one person. And don't be put off by the thought of all that measuring out. It may seem a chore at first, but you only need to do it until you're used to visualizing how much you need. You don't need to stick rigidly to my serving suggestions, either. If you feel like trying a new salad dressing or sauce, turn to my recipes on pages 16 and 17.

Type of food	amount	cooking method	grams of fat	of which saturates
Dried pasta	4 oz / 125 g	boiled	0.7 g	0.1 g
Long-grain rice	4 oz / 125 g	boiled	0.3 g	0.1 g
Potato	7 oz / 200 g	baked	0.2 g	0.1 g
Sweet potato	5 oz / 150 g	baked	0.5 g	0.1 g

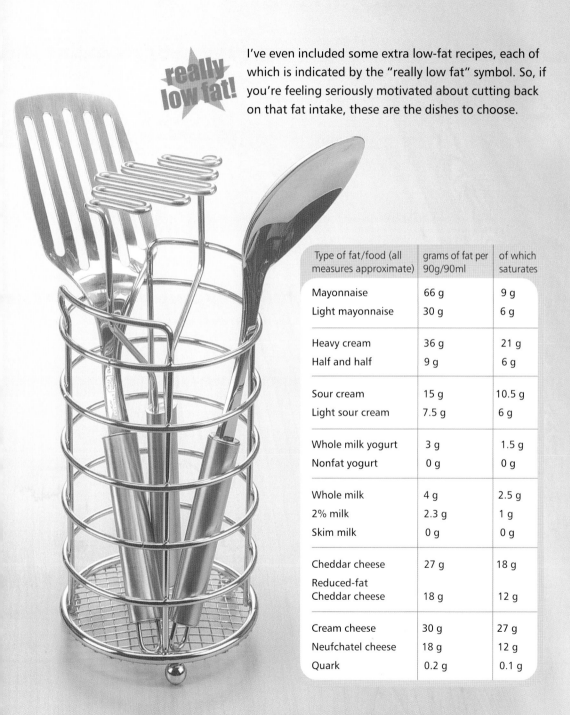

really low fat!

I've even included some extra low-fat recipes, each of which is indicated by the "really low fat" symbol. So, if you're feeling seriously motivated about cutting back on that fat intake, these are the dishes to choose.

Type of fat/food (all measures approximate)	grams of fat per 90g/90ml	of which saturates
Mayonnaise	66 g	9 g
Light mayonnaise	30 g	6 g
Heavy cream	36 g	21 g
Half and half	9 g	6 g
Sour cream	15 g	10.5 g
Light sour cream	7.5 g	6 g
Whole milk yogurt	3 g	1.5 g
Nonfat yogurt	0 g	0 g
Whole milk	4 g	2.5 g
2% milk	2.3 g	1 g
Skim milk	0 g	0 g
Cheddar cheese	27 g	18 g
Reduced-fat Cheddar cheese	18 g	12 g
Cream cheese	30 g	27 g
Neufchatel cheese	18 g	12 g
Quark	0.2 g	0.1 g

Ainsley's top tips for low-fat eating

To show you just how easy it is to cut down on fat, here are my top tips for low-fat eating. Many of them are easy to do and really just call for you to use your common sense—they don't involve huge changes in your lifestyle.

1 Eat more fruit and vegetables: Look at the dessert section of this book and hunt out all those fabulous fruit smoothie recipes to start off your day with an energy-packed breakfast drink.

2 Watch what you eat: If you decide to splurge on a full breakfast that you know is higher in fat than you need, then have a lighter lunch or dinner dish to help compensate later on.

3 Use an oil spray—there is less than 1 calorie in each spray of oil, and you'll be surprised by how little you need.

4 Exercise: Oohhhh, yes, diet and exercise come hand in hand. It doesn't mean you have to run around a field all day. You could walk the kids to school; it all counts.

5 Choose lean cuts of meat, select skinless chicken breast and trim any visible fat from lean pork, beef, or ham. Serve grilled fish, meat, or chicken with one of my low-fat sauces or salsas (see pages 16–17) instead of heavy sauces.

6 Choose fresh garnishes, such as herbs or arugula. Thin a little plain yogurt with milk and use this blend rather than high-fat sauces to drizzle over dishes.

7 Use canned tuna in water rather than oil, semi-dried tomatoes rather than sun-dried tomatoes (which are often packed in oil), and marinated olives in a pickled brine.

8 Eat plenty of leafy salad with vegetables such as fresh tomatoes, cucumber, corn, radishes, and other low-fat vegetables. The dressing adds most of the fat, so try one of my fat-free dressings on pages 16–17.

9 Drink plenty of fluids—these can be spread across hot and cold beverages. However, try to make more than half your intake water and try to cut down on tea and coffee. You should be drinking eight glasses of liquid each day..

10 Once you start experimenting, you'll quickly see how you can adjust the flavors of dishes simply by adding more chopped fresh herbs or seasoning with soy sauce.

Cooking up a storm

Some cooking methods are much healthier than others. I have used a wide variety of techniques when putting together the recipes in this book, but I have avoided deep- and shallow frying as they are sure ways to take in more fat than you need. Instead, try the techniques below—some of them are even fat free. Use them when you're preparing your favorite dishes at home and you'll be amazed at how easily you cut back on fat.

• **Stir-frying**: You need much less oil and the method of cooking is quick, allowing a lot less fat to be absorbed into the food. Cut all your ingredients into even-sized pieces to ensure even cooking. If your mixture looks too dry, add a splash of water, soy sauce, or hot sauce or, if you are using noodles, a couple of tablespoons of the cooking water.

• **Steaming**: Get steamed! It is the healthiest way to cook vegetables and keeps all those important water-soluble vitamins inside, which are so easily lost through other cooking methods. If you don't have a steamer, don't worry. You can buy a collapsible version that will fit nicely into a pot, or try a bamboo steamer from your local ethnic grocer.

• **Microwaving**: Many of us have microwaves in our kitchen, mainly because they are so useful for saving time when we're cooking in a hurry. However, what many people don't realize is that they are also a great way to cook without using any fat. Vegetables can simply be sprinkled with a little water and steamed in the microwave, retaining all those wonderful nutrients and vitamins that we need to keep us healthy. Onions can be softened with water and a tiny bit of butter for flavor. I also like to use microwaves to cook delicate fish—it really is a great idea for a quick, healthy supper. One of the best ways to do this is to cook the fish *en papillote* (in paper). Try my recipe for Baked Cantonese Cod Corners on page 62—in the microwave the fish will cook in less than four minutes! Make sure you wrap the fish in waxed paper or baking parchment rather than foil, as you could seriously damage your microwave with metal.

• **Broiling or grilling**: Whether you use your broiler, an outdoor grill, an electric grill, or a grill pan, these are excellent ways to cook meat, fish, and even a few desserts! I use a spray bottle of oil (you can find these in supermarkets) that evenly coats ingredients with a tiny bit of oil. Marinating meats and fish before broiling or grilling not only packs in the flavor, but also keeps them moist and tender while they are cooking.

• **Roasting**: This is a great low-fat way to cook meats, poultry, and fish. After you've roasted the meat, skim the fat off the surface to leave the pan juices virtually fat free for a tasty gravy. Roasting also caramelizes the natural sugars in vegetables, giving them a wonderful flavor. Try adding roasted vegetables to salads or sandwiches for a tasty lunchtime snack.

Don't panic, you can live a little!

Many people are worried that if they start to watch what they eat they'll have to miss out on all those treats that make eating fun, like sauces, dips, and dressings. But I don't believe that we should have to compromise on flavor, so take a look at my low-fat accompaniments for fish, meat, and salads. The salsas are packed with flavor and the suggestions for low-fat gravies would work perfectly with a delicious Sunday lunch. Why not try them out on the family?

ITALIAN TOMATO SALSA

Cut 6 ripe, skinned and seeded *plum tomatoes* into thin strips. Remove the stalks from a small bunch of *basil leaves* and very finely shred. Stir into the tomatoes with about 12 small (25 g) thinly sliced, pitted *black olives*, 3 very finely chopped *shallots*, 2 very finely chopped *garlic cloves*, 1 tablespoon *olive oil,* and 2–3 teaspoons *balsamic vinegar*. Season to taste with *salt* and freshly ground *black pepper*.

Serves 8

2 g fat per serving

CITRUS AND GINGER DRESSING

Whisk together 2 tablespoons *sugar*, 1 tablespoon *ginger syrup* (taken from a jar of preserved ginger or bought at a coffee shop), 2 tablespoons *orange juice* and 2 teaspoons *lemon juice*. Season to taste with *salt* and freshly ground *black pepper*.

Serves 3–4

0 g fat per serving

CRANBERRY AND RED WINE GRAVY

Pour 1 bottle *red wine* into a large saucepan. Add 2 sliced *shallots*, 3 cloves crushed *garlic,* and 1 sprig of *rosemary*. Bring to a boil and boil rapidly for about 10–12 minutes until reduced by half. Whisk in 6 tablespoons *cranberry sauce* and 2–3 teaspoons *sugar* to taste. Discard the rosemary. Season with *salt* and freshly ground *black pepper*.

Serves 3–4

0.1 g fat per serving

Puréed fruit sweetened with confectioners' sugar makes a great topping for desserts.

MANGO AND PINEAPPLE SALSA

Slice off the top and bottom of a *baby pineapple*. Slice away the skin and the little brown eyes. Cut into quarters and remove and discard the core. Cut the flesh into small dice and stir in 1 small peeled, pitted, and diced ripe *mango*, 5 thinly sliced *scallions*, 1 seeded and finely chopped *red hot pepper*, 3 tablespoons *lime juice*, 1 tablespoon fresh chopped *mint,* and *salt* and freshly ground *pepper* to taste.

Serves 8

0.1 g fat per serving

LOW-FAT BLUE CHEESE DRESSING

Simply crumble 2 tablespoons (25 g) *blue cheese* into a blender, add 4 tablespoons of *reduced-fat sour cream*, 2 teaspoons *white wine vinegar,* and blend until smooth and creamy. Season to taste with *salt* and freshly ground *black pepper*.

Serves 4

4.1 g fat per serving

Be adventurous and try sushi for a tasty low-fat snack.

TOMATO VINAIGRETTE

Skin and seed 2 large, ripe *plum tomatoes* and roughly chop the flesh. Place into a blender with 1 small peeled *garlic clove*, a small handful of *basil,* and a good splash of *balsamic vinegar*. Squeeze over the juice of half a small *lime* and add 5 tablespoons *vegetable stock*. Blend until smooth. Season to taste with *salt* and freshly ground *black pepper*.

Makes 150 ml (¼ pint)

0.1 g fat per serving

ONION AND CIDER GRAVY

Melt 1 tablespoon (15 g) *butter* in a large saucepan and sauté 1 large *onion*, cut into thin wedges for 3–4 minutes until softened. Add 3 cloves crushed *garlic* and fry for 1–2 minutes. Pour in 1¼ cups (300 ml) *dry cider* (or *dry white wine* or *vermouth*), bring to a boil and simmer for 5–6 minutes. Add 2 cups (450 ml) *vegetable stock* and bring to a boil. Mix 2 tablespoons *cornstarch* with 4 table-spoons *water* to a smooth paste and whisk into the cider gravy. Continue whisking until the gravy is thick and glossy. Season well with freshly ground *black pepper*, to taste.

Serves 3–4

4.3 g fat per serving

For an extra-low-fat salad dressing, toss the salad in freshly squeezed orange juice flavored with a little mustard.

Soups,

Red lentil soup with lemon yogurt

Thai lemongrass, chicken, and
mushroom broth

Caramelized onion soup

Minty spinach, garlic, and
nutmeg soup

Roasted tomato, thyme, and crème
fraîche soup

starters, and snacks

Celeriac, orange, and saffron soup

Baked shrimp and hot-pepper
ginger cakes

No-need-to-cook hoisin spring rolls

Kufta kebabs with hot-pepper
yogurt

Hot-smoked-salmon pâté

Louisiana blue cheese and chicken
sandwich

Virtually fat-free falafels

Bang bang tofu lettuce wraps

Red lentil soup with lemon yogurt

Nutrition notes per serving:

★ calories 171
★ protein 11 g
★ carbohydrate 24 g
★ fat 4 g
★ saturated fat none
★ fiber 3 g
★ added sugar none
★ salt 1.33 g

This delicious and substantial vegetarian soup is a perfect warming dish for a cold winter night. To prepare ahead, make the soup up to the end of step 2, then cool it thoroughly and freeze for up to 1 month. Defrost thoroughly before reheating and completing the soup.

Preparation: 10 minutes • Cooking time: 35–40 minutes • Serves 4

1 tablespoon olive oil
1 onion, finely chopped
leaves from 1 sprig fresh thyme
2 carrots, finely diced
2 garlic cloves, finely chopped
1 red hot pepper, seeded and finely diced
1 teaspoon yellow mustard seeds
3 tomatoes, roughly diced
¾ cup (100 g) red lentils
5 cups (1.2 liters) hot vegetable stock
4 tablespoons nonfat plain yogurt
finely grated zest and juice of 1 small lemon
salt and freshly ground black pepper

1 Heat the oil in a large pan and cook the onion, thyme, and carrots for about 3–4 minutes until the vegetables begin to soften. Add the garlic, hot pepper, and mustard seeds and cook for a couple of minutes more.

2 Stir in the tomatoes, lentils, and stock, and bring to a boil. Reduce the heat, cover, and simmer gently for 30 minutes until the lentils are tender and easy to crush.

3 Mix together the yogurt and half of the lemon zest, and season to taste. Squeeze the lemon juice into the soup and season with salt and pepper.

4 Ladle the soup into warmed serving bowls and serve with a spoonful of the lemon yogurt, scattered with the remaining lemon zest and some freshly ground black pepper.

The red lentils are used to make a thick and tasty base for this soup. Alternatively, you could use yellow split peas (but beware—these do need soaking overnight before using).

Thai lemongrass, chicken, and mushroom broth

With many of the ingredients used in Thai cooking now readily available, authentic Thai soups are easy to make. My recipe features lean chicken, but you could also try making the soup with shrimp, diced or minced pork, or, for an extra-low-fat version, extra vegetables.

Preparation: 10 minutes • Cooking time: 15 minutes • Serves 2

1 lemongrass stalk
2¼ cups (600 ml) hot chicken stock
2 skinless, boneless chicken breasts, diced
1–2 teaspoons Thai red curry paste (see below)
1 shallot, finely chopped
½ cup (100 g) shiitake mushrooms, sliced, or canned straw mushrooms, halved

2 teaspoons light brown sugar
1 teaspoon Thai fish sauce (nam pla)
juice of 1 lemon
salt and freshly ground black pepper
To serve
1 scallion, thinly sliced
1 red hot pepper, thinly sliced
handful of cilantro

1 Flatten the lemongrass stalk with a rolling pin or meat mallet and place in a pan with the stock, chicken, curry paste, and shallot; bring to a boil. Add the mushrooms to the pan and simmer gently for 8–10 minutes.

2 Stir the sugar and fish sauce into the soup and simmer for 3 minutes until the chicken is cooked. Squeeze in the lemon juice and season to taste.

3 Ladle the soup into warmed serving bowls and scatter over the scallion, hot pepper, and coriander. Serve with an extra wedge of lemon, if liked.

MAKE YOUR OWN … Store-bought Thai curry pastes have a lot of oil in them to give them a longer shelf life. Here's my own low-fat version. Put **1 small roughly chopped red onion, 4 garlic cloves, a 2-inch (5-cm) piece peeled and roughly chopped fresh ginger or galangal, 6 red Thai hot peppers** (remove seeds for a milder flavor) and **1 lemongrass stalk** (tough outer leaves removed and inner stalk roughly chopped) into a food processor and process to a coarse paste. Add **1/2 teaspoon salt, 1 teaspoon coriander seeds, and the juice and finely grated rind of 1 lime,** and purée until smooth. Keep in a screw-top jar in the refrigerator for up to 2 weeks.

For a lovely winter warmer that will keep the chill at bay, stir a handful of shredded ginger into the broth.

People have given me lots of suggestions for keeping my eyes from watering when I'm chopping onions: wearing sunglasses, whistling, chewing parsley, or chilling the onions before slicing them. What do you do?

Caramelized onion soup

Nutrition notes
per serving:

★ calories 297
★ protein 6 g
★ carbohydrate 34 g
★ fat 11 g
★ saturated fat 7 g
★ fiber 4 g
★ added sugar 8 g
★ salt 1.48 g

This version of the French classic is just right for a light lunch. Cook the onions slowly over medium heat, so that the natural sugars caramelize for that wonderful rich flavor. Don't be tempted to caramelize them too quickly, though, as they will burn, leaving you with bitter-tasting soup.

Preparation: 10 minutes • Cooking time: 35–40 minutes • Serves 2

2 tablespoons (25 g) butter
3 large Spanish onions, thinly sliced
1 tablespoon sugar
2 garlic cloves, crushed
⅔ cup (150 ml) dry white wine

2¼ cups (600 ml) hot chicken or
   vegetable stock
1 tablespoon Worcestershire sauce
1 tablespoon French brandy
   (optional but dee-lish)

1 Melt the butter in a large pan and add the sliced onions. Sprinkle in the sugar and cook over medium heat for 10–12 minutes, stirring frequently until you get a lovely caramel-brown tinge to your onions. Add the garlic and cook for 30 seconds more.

2 Pour the wine into the pan and cook vigorously for 1–2 minutes. Stir in the stock and Worcestershire sauce, bring to a boil, reduce the heat, and simmer for 15–20 minutes until the onions are tender. Stir in the brandy, if using, and divide between warmed serving bowls. Serve topped with thin slices of toasted French bread.

Minty spinach, garlic, and nutmeg soup

This simple soup is bursting with fresh flavor and the color is certainly vibrant. It's pure health in a bowl—packed full of goodness. To save yourself a lot of time, buy tender or young spinach leaves that need no preparation. Simply use them straight from the bag.

Preparation: 15 minutes • Cooking time: 30 minutes • Serves 4

1 tablespoon olive oil
2 large onions, roughly chopped
2 garlic cloves, roughly chopped
1 small red hot pepper, finely chopped
1 bunch fresh mint, roughly chopped
1 bunch fresh parsley or cilantro, roughly chopped
5 cups (1.2 liters) hot vegetable stock
18 oz (500 g) fresh young spinach, roughly chopped
juice of 1–2 lemons
Pinch of ground nutmeg
salt and freshly ground black pepper
low-fat plain yogurt and crusty bread, to serve (optional)

1 Heat the oil in a large pan and cook the onions, garlic, and hot pepper for 10 minutes until softened and golden. Add the herbs and stock, bring to a boil and simmer for 15 minutes.

2 Add the spinach to the pan and cook for 2 minutes until just wilted. Add the lemon juice, nutmeg, and salt and pepper to taste. Using a hand blender, purée the soup. Ladle into warmed serving bowls, drizzle with the yogurt, if liked, and dust with fresh black pepper. Serve with crusty bread.

Don't make this soup too far ahead of time—although it will still taste great, its lovely bright green color fades quickly.

Roasted tomato, thyme, and crème fraîche soup

Roasting the tomatoes really intensifies their flavor. Yes, this recipe does contain a whole head of garlic—ooh, lovely, especially on a first date! However, cooking garlic in this way makes it sweeter and milder, and it is not so harsh on the palate.

Preparation: 30 minutes • Cooking time: 45 minutes • Serves 4

8 large ripe tomatoes, halved
1 red onion, unpeeled and cut into quarters
1 head garlic, halved horizontally
2 sprigs thyme
1 tablespoon olive oil
4 cups (1 litre) hot vegetable stock

½ cup (100 g) reduced-fat crème fraîche or reduced-fat sour cream
3 tablespoons chopped fresh parsley
sea salt and freshly ground black pepper
warm crusty bread, to serve (optional)

1 Preheat the oven to 400°F/200°C. Place the tomatoes, onion, garlic, and thyme in a roasting pan and drizzle with oil. Season generously and roast for 30 minutes until softened and a little charred.

2 Remove the onion quarters and garlic from the roasting pan and set aside. Pour half the stock over the tomatoes and return to the oven for 10 minutes.

3 Meanwhile, slip the onion quarters and garlic out of their papery skins and use a food processor to turn them into a paste.

4 Remove the roasting pan from the oven, discard the thyme sprigs, then add the stock and tomatoes to the food processor, scraping up any residue with a wooden spoon. Process until smooth.

5 Strain the mixture into a clean pan and add the remaining stock and the crème fraîche. Heat gently and season to taste. Stir in the parsley, ladle into warmed serving bowls, and serve with warm, crusty bread.

Celeriac, orange, and saffron soup

A velvety soup with loads of flavor that's easy to make and totally satisfying. To prepare celeriac, also called celery root, just cut off the fibrous skin to reveal the white flesh underneath. I think that celeriac is an underrated vegetable; try it baked with potatoes and onions for a tasty accompaniment.

Preparation: 15 minutes • Cooking time: 40 minutes • Serves 6

1 tablespoon olive oil
1 large onion, chopped
1 garlic clove, crushed
1 celeriac, about 20 oz (600 g),
  peeled and cut into ¾-inch (2-cm)
  chunks
4 medium potatoes, about 21 oz
  (600 g), cut into chunks

6 cups (1.5 liters) hot vegetable stock
large pinch saffron strands
finely grated zest and juice of
  2 large oranges
salt and freshly ground black pepper
fresh flat-leaf parsley sprigs, to
  garnish

1 Heat the oil in a large pan and fry the onion for 3–4 minutes until softened. Add the garlic, celeriac, and potatoes. Cover and cook, stirring occasionally, for 10 minutes (adding a little water if the vegetables begin to stick).

2 Add the stock, saffron, and orange juice. Bring to a boil and simmer for 20 minutes until the vegetables are tender.

3 Purée in batches until smooth, return to a clean pan, and heat through. Season with salt and pepper to taste.

4 Divide the soup between warmed serving bowls. Scatter with orange zest and flat-leaf parsley to garnish.

Baked shrimp and hot-pepper ginger cakes

Nutrition notes
per serving:

★ calories 140
★ protein 16 g
★ carbohydrate 13 g
★ fat 3 g
★ saturated fat 1 g
★ fiber 1 g
★ added sugar none
★ salt 1.94 g

All those delicious Thai flavors wrapped up in these soft, fluffy cakes! For an extra burst of flavor, serve drizzled with my sweet chili sauce or a squeeze of fresh lime juice. If you're having a party and looking for some low-fat canapés, these make great tasty nibbles.

Preparation: 15 minutes • Cooking time: 15–20 minutes • Serves 4 (makes 12)

2 thick slices white bread, crusts removed
9 oz (250 g) peeled raw shrimp (about 20 medium)
1 green hot pepper, seeded and finely chopped
1-inch (2.5-cm) piece fresh ginger, peeled and finely chopped
4 garlic cloves, finely chopped
1 tablespoon chopped cilantro
1 teaspoon salt
1 egg
oil, for spraying
To serve
baby lettuce leaves, arugula, or watercress
sweet chili sauce (see below)

1 Place the bread in a bowl, cover with water, soak for about 10 seconds, then squeeze out excess water. Place the drained bread in a food processor with the shrimp, hot pepper, ginger, garlic, cilantro, salt, and egg. Pulse until well blended.

2 Preheat the oven to 400°F/200°C. Using lightly floured hands, divide the mixture into 12 small cakes. Spray the oil very lightly onto a baking sheet and arrange the shrimp cakes on the baking sheet, evenly spaced. Spray with a little oil and bake for 15–20 minutes, turning halfway through, until golden brown and just beginning to crisp. Serve warm with baby lettuce, arugula, or watercress leaves and a bowl of sweet chili sauce.

MAKE YOUR OWN … Sweet chili sauce is wonderful with these little shrimp cakes, and here's my low-fat version. Put **1 chopped onion, 2 finely chopped garlic cloves, 2 finely chopped red hot peppers, and the juice of 1 orange** into a small pan. Bring to a boil and simmer very gently for 4–5 minutes until the onions are softened and the orange juice nearly all absorbed. Stir in the **juice of another orange, 1 tablespoon honey, 1 tablespoon malt vinegar or red wine vinegar, and 2 tablespoons tomato ketchup.** Bring back to the boil and simmer very gently for 2–3 minutes until thickened. Serve warm.

No-need-to-cook hoisin spring rolls

Nutrition notes
per serving:

★ calories 212
★ protein 28 g
★ carbohydrate 17 g
★ fat 4 g
★ saturated fat 1 g
★ fiber 1 g
★ added sugar 3 g
★ salt 0.86 g

Most large supermarkets now stock oriental ingredients, such as rice-paper wrappers. Keep wrappers on hand; they are great for a last-minute starter or snack—all you do is soak them in hot water and then fill with your favorite ingredients. Be careful when handling them as they tear easily.

Preparation: 20 minutes • Cooking time: none • Serves 4

twelve 3 x 6 inch (7.5 x 15 cm)
  rice-paper wrappers
1 carrot, cut into matchsticks
3-inch (7.5-cm) piece cucumber
4 scallions, shredded

1 tablespoon sesame seeds
4 tablespoons hoisin sauce
small bunch of cilantro
12 oz (350 g) lean cooked chicken,
  shredded (about 2 large breasts)

1 Place the rice-paper wrappers in a heatproof bowl and cover with hot water; soak for 5 minutes until soft and pliable.

2 In a separate bowl, toss together the carrot, cucumber, scallions, and sesame seeds.

3 Drain the rice papers on a clean dish towel and spread 1 teaspoon of the hoisin sauce across the center of each. Sprinkle with a few cilantro leaves. Place the vegetables and then the chicken on top. Make sure you don't overfill the papers; they may split if you do.

4 Fold 2 sides in, then roll up to make a neat cylindrical shape. Serve immediately with extra hoisin sauce for dipping.

The spring rolls are not at their best if made too far ahead of time. Instead, prepare the vegetables and the chicken, cover separately, and chill until ready to use.

Kufta kebabs with hot-pepper yogurt

Nutrition notes
per serving:

★ calories 296
★ protein 31 g
★ carbohydrate 24 g
★ fat 9 g
★ saturated fat 4 g
★ fiber 2 g
★ added sugar 1 g
★ salt 0.8 g

Watch for extra-lean ground lamb in your supermarket, or ask for it at your butcher's. Remember to soak the wooden skewers for 20 minutes before you start to prepare your tasty kuftas. You'll get those taste buds tingling with my hot-pepper yogurt—watch out, it has a mighty kick!

Preparation: 15 minutes • Cooking time: 15 minutes • Serves 4

1 lb (450 g) extra-lean ground lamb
1 small white onion, finely chopped
1 tablespoon chopped fresh mint
1 tablespoon chopped fresh parsley
1 teaspoon chopped fresh rosemary
½ teaspoon each mixed spice, ground coriander, and ground cumin
4 flour tortillas
1 red onion, thinly sliced into rings (optional)
salt and freshly ground black pepper

For the hot-pepper yogurt
8 oz (200 g) carton nonfat plain yogurt
2 red hot peppers, seeded and finely chopped
2 tablespoons chopped cilantro
1 garlic clove, crushed
juice of 1 lime
pinch sugar
tomato wedges, lettuce leaves, and a wedge of lime, to serve.

1 Preheat the grill to high. Mix together the lamb, white onion, herbs, and spices and season with salt and pepper. Divide the mixture into 4 parts and, using your fingers, squeeze it around skewers to form long sausage shapes.

2 Grill the kufta kebabs for 10–12 minutes, turning occasionally, until well browned but still a little pink in the center.

3 Make the hot-pepper yogurt: Combine the yogurt, hot peppers, cilantro, garlic, lime juice, and sugar, and season to taste.

4 Briefly warm the tortillas for a few seconds on each side in a dry, nonstick frying pan, or for 10 seconds in a microwave, to make them soft and pliable. Place a kebab in the center of each tortilla and squeeze the tortilla around the kebab, pulling it off the skewer. Scatter with a few onion rings and drizzle over the hot-pepper yogurt. Serve with the tomato wedges, crisp lettuce leaves, and a wedge of lime to squeeze over.

Hot-smoked-salmon pâté

Nutrition notes
per serving:

★ calories 341
★ protein 45 g
★ carbohydrate 19 g
★ fat 10 g
★ saturated fat 2 g
★ fiber 1 g
★ added sugar none
★ salt 6.5 g

You don't have to go all the way to New York to get my favorite deli sandwich, although here I serve the hot-smoked-salmon pâté with toasted ciabatta rolls instead of the traditional bagel. Hot-smoked salmon is now available in larger supermarkets and specialty food stores.

Preparation: 15 minutes • Cooking time: 5 minutes • Serves 4

2 teaspoons olive oil
4 scallions, thinly sliced
18 oz (500 g) hot-smoked salmon, skinned and boned
8 oz (250 g) carton Quark (low-fat soft cheese, available at health-food stores)

1 teaspoon creamed horseradish
dash Tabasco
freshly ground black pepper
2 small ciabatta rolls
1 scallion, sliced, and lemon wedges for serving (optional)

1 Heat the oil in a pan and sauté the scallions for 1 minute. Flake in the fish, then beat well, cooking for a minute or two more. Remove from the heat—if the mixture gets too hot, let cool slightly.

2 Add the Quark, horseradish, Tabasco, and black pepper, and mix together until well combined.

3 Thinly slice the ciabatta rolls and lightly toast them. Serve with the hot-smoked-salmon pâté and if you like, a sprinkling of thinly sliced scallions and lemon wedges to squeeze over.

The hot-smoked salmon is naturally salty, so don't add extra salt. Try this recipe with hot-smoked trout as well.

Use different types of bread—French bread or pita are equally delicious.

Louisiana blue cheese and chicken sandwich

Nutrition notes
per serving:

★ calories 345
★ protein 38 g
★ carbohydrate 33 g
★ fat 10 g
★ saturated fat 4 g
★ fiber 2 g
★ added sugar none
★ salt 1.84 g

Feelin' hot, hot, hot? This tasty chicken sandwich is my best-ever late-night Cajun snack. I raid my fridge and throw in whatever takes my fancy. I usually add a splash of Tabasco sauce for that extra burst of heat. To reduce the fat even more, leave out the blue-cheese mayonnaise.

Preparation: 10 minutes • Cooking time: 15 minutes • Serves 1

1 skinless, boneless chicken breast
1 teaspoon Cajun seasoning or
  ½ teaspoon Chinese five-spice
  powder and a pinch cayenne
  pepper
juice of ½ lemon (optional)
1 tablespoon (15 g) crumbled
  blue cheese

1 teaspoon low-fat mayonnaise
4 cherry tomatoes, halved, or
  1 small tomato, sliced
1 scallion, sliced, or a few dice of
  raw onion
handful of lettuce leaves
2 slices bread or 2 large pita pockets
salt and freshly ground black pepper

1 Season the chicken with spice, salt, and pepper. Cook in a nonstick frying pan for 5 minutes, then turn and cook for about 4 minutes, until cooked through but still moist and juicy. Now squeeze over a little lemon juice, if you like.

2 While the chicken is cooking, mash together the blue cheese and mayonnaise.

3 Layer the salad ingredients on top of one of the slices of bread or inside the warmed split pita pockets and top with moist chicken, followed by the blue-cheese mayonnaise. Sandwich together and eat warm.

Virtually fat-free falafels

Nutrition notes
per serving:

★ calories 214
★ protein 14 g
★ carbohydrate 30 g
★ fat 5 g
★ saturated fat 1.6 g
★ fiber 6 g
★ added sugar none
★ salt 1.7 g

Don't be tempted to use canned chick peas for this recipe. It is worth the extra cooking time to use dried and cook them yourself—the texture is truly excellent. Serve them in a warm pita pocket with yogurt and crispy salad ingredients. They're guaranteed to be received with mouthwatering acclaim.

Preparation: 15 minutes + overnight soaking • Cooking time: 15 minutes • Serves 4 (makes 16 falafels)

1 cup (225 g) dried chick peas,
 soaked overnight in water
1 teaspoon salt
1 teaspoon cumin seeds
1 teaspoon ground coriander
½ teaspoon cayenne pepper
1 garlic clove, crushed
2 tablespoons chopped fresh parsley

juice of ½ lemon
1 egg
oil, for spraying
To serve
4 pita breads, mixed salad greens,
 and low-fat plain yogurt
cherry tomatoes (optional)

1 Drain the chick peas and place in a pan, cover with fresh water, bring to a boil, and boil rapidly for 20 minutes. Drain and place in a food processor with the salt, cumin, coriander, cayenne, garlic, parsley, lemon juice, and egg. Process until very finely chopped but not puréed. (If you have time, set the mixture aside for a couple of hours so that the flavors can mingle, but it's not imperative.)

2 Preheat the oven to 425°F/220°C. Using wet hands, shape the mixture into 16 balls, then flatten slightly into patties. Spray the oil very lightly onto a baking sheet and arrange the falafels, evenly spaced. Spray lightly with oil and bake for 15–20 minutes.

3 Place 4 falafels inside each warm pita bread with mixed salad greens and cherry tomatoes, if liked. Serve the low-fat yogurt in a separate bowl to drizzle over the top.

Bang bang tofu lettuce wraps

Nutrition notes
per serving:

★ calories 175
★ protein 9 g
★ carbohydrate 18 g
★ fat 7 g
★ saturated fat 1 g
★ fiber 2 g
★ added sugar 9 g
★ salt 2.77 g

These tasty bundles of hot and spicy stir-fried tofu wrapped in cool, crisp lettuce leaves make a mouthwatering treat. If your store sells it, use pre-marinated tofu (sometimes called "baked" tofu); it tastes good to begin with and acts like a sponge, soaking up all those wonderful flavors. If you prefer, marinate your own tofu in fat-free salad dressing.

Preparation: 10 minutes + marinating time • Cooking time: 5 minutes • Serves 4

4 tablespoons soy sauce
1 teaspoon Chinese five-spice powder
3 tablespoons honey
3 tablespoons sherry
2-inch (5-cm) piece fresh ginger, peeled and finely grated
2 red hot peppers, seeded and thinly sliced

10 oz (300 g) pre-marinated or baked tofu pieces
1 small iceberg lettuce
1 tablespoon sesame oil
2 carrots, cut into matchsticks
½ small cucumber, cut into matchsticks
1 cup (200 g) bean sprouts
small handful of chopped cilantro

1 Mix together the soy sauce, Chinese five-spice powder, honey, sherry, ginger, hot peppers, and tofu. Toss well and marinate for 30 minutes.

2 Meanwhile, remove 4 outer leaves from the lettuce. Rinse in cold water, shake off any excess, and chill for 30 minutes.

3 Heat the oil in a wok. Lift the tofu out of the marinade and stir-fry over high heat for 2 minutes. Add the carrots and stir-fry for 2 minutes more. Remove from heat and stir in cucumber, bean sprouts, and cilantro. Put the lettuce leaves on 4 plates and divide the tofu mixture between them. Wrap each leaf around the filling and serve immediately with extra soy sauce for splashing or dipping, if liked.

Fresh

Fresh tuna burgers with
red-onion salsa

Sinhalese linguine shrimp pasta

Jalapeño tiger-shrimp ginger
skewers

Shrimp, mushroom, and bean
sprout noodles

Roasted lemon bay-scented
cod

Classic moules marinière

Glazed monkfish skewers with
udon noodles

and tasty fish

Baked Cantonese cod corners

Light and crunchy fish cakes

Cod kebab zingers with
salsa tagliatelle

Seared squid with citrus
mango salad

Charred tuna with green
lentil salad

Fresh tuna burgers with red-onion salsa

Nutrition notes
per serving:

★ calories 348
★ protein 30 g
★ carbohydrate 33 g
★ fat 11 g
★ saturated fat 2 g
★ fiber 2 g
★ added sugar none
★ salt 1.87 g

I've added wasabi, which is Japanese horseradish, to these burgers because it gives such a fantastic kick. You will find wasabi in the Asian or ethnic sections of large supermarkets, but if you can't get hold of it, a dab of good mustard will do.

Preparation: 25 minutes +1 hour standing time • Cooking time: 15 minutes • Serves 4

For the salsa
1 red onion, finely diced
2 plum tomatoes, seeded and chopped
1 green hot pepper, seeded and
  finely chopped
juice of 1 lime
2 teaspoons olive oil
salt and freshly ground black pepper

For the burgers
1 lb (450 g) fresh tuna
1–2 teaspoons wasabi paste
1 tablespoon sesame seeds
oil, for spraying
1 ciabatta loaf, sliced and toasted
lime slices, to garnish

1 Begin by making the salsa: Stir all the ingredients together and set aside at room temperature for at least an hour to allow the flavors to infuse.

2 Place the tuna in a food processor and pulse until coarsely minced. Transfer to a bowl and mix with the wasabi paste, sesame seeds, and some salt and pepper. With damp hands, shape the mixture into 4 even-sized burgers.

3 Preheat the oven to 400°F/200°C. Spray a baking sheet with a little oil and arrange the burgers on the tray. Spray with a little more oil and bake for 15 minutes until golden brown and just cooked through.

4 Place the tuna burgers on the toasted ciabatta slices and top with a dollop of salsa. Garnish with the slices of fresh lime and serve warm.

Sinhalese linguine shrimp pasta

Sometimes the meals that are quick and easy are the best, and are the ones you return to time and again. This is a wonderful meal that's ready in 20 minutes from start to finish! Try using spaghetti or noodles for a change, and if you're not into fish, marinated tofu is delicious instead of shrimp.

Preparation: 10 minutes • Cooking time: 8–10 minutes • Serves 2

1 lb (450 g) linguine
2 teaspoons olive oil
½ small onion, peeled and finely
  chopped
1 garlic clove, crushed
1 tablespoon curry paste
1 tablespoon chopped cilantro,
  plus extra to garnish

1 tablespoon chopped fresh mint
1 tablespoon chopped fresh parsley
8 oz (225 g) peeled shrimp
  (about 20 medium)
grated zest and juice of 1 lemon
salt and freshly ground black pepper

1 Cook the linguine in a large pan of boiling water, salted if you wish, following the package cooking instructions. When the pasta is al dente (tender but still offering some resistance to the bite), remove from the heat and drain, reserving 12 tablespoons of the cooking water.

2 Heat the oil in a large frying pan or wok, add the onion and garlic, and fry without allowing them to brown. Add the curry paste and stir-fry for 20 seconds, then throw in the cooking water, all the herbs, shrimp, and lemon zest. Toss to heat through, then squeeze in the lemon juice. Lightly season.

3 Toss the cooked pasta with the curried shrimp mixture and serve garnished with cilantro leaves.

Jalapeño tiger-shrimp ginger skewers

Nutrition notes per serving:

- ★ calories 126
- ★ protein 22 g
- ★ carbohydrate 2 g
- ★ fat 2 g
- ★ saturated fat 2 g
- ★ fiber none
- ★ added sugar none
- ★ salt 1.14 g

I first made these in Key West, overlooking the waters of the Gulf of Mexico. The locals were so impressed that their barbie bar now has them on its menu. I use jalapeño peppers for this dish because they have a delicate flavor. Try to get a variety of colors—red, green, and yellow.

Preparation: 15 minutes • Cooking time: 5 minutes • Serves 4

12 red jalapeño peppers
12 green jalapeño peppers
12 fresh basil leaves, finely shredded
1½-inch (4-cm) piece fresh ginger, peeled and finely chopped

24 raw tiger shrimp
1 tablespoon (15g) butter
salt and freshly ground black pepper
lemon or lime wedges, to serve

1 Slit open the jalapeños from top to bottom, taking care to leave the stalks intact. Scrape out the seeds. Divide the shredded basil and chopped ginger between the jalapeños and generously season the jalapeños inside.

2 Shell the shrimp, leaving the tail section intact. Place a whole shrimp inside each jalapeño, leaving the tail poking out of the pointed end. Smear a dab of butter on top of each shrimp, then squeeze the jalapeño together to enclose the shrimp.

3 Thread 3 jalapeños, alternating the colors, onto 2 short, parallel bamboo skewers so that the jalapeños look like the rungs of a ladder. (You will need to soak the skewers for 20 minutes before using them.) Repeat to make 8 ladders.

4 Cook the jalapeños over fairly hot coals for about 5 minutes, turning frequently until they are softened and a little charred, and the shrimp are cooked through. Serve with wedges of lemon or lime. Delicious.

You can still make these skewers if you don't have an outdoor grill. Just cook them under a hot broiler for 7–8 minutes, turning frequently.

Shrimp, mushroom, and bean sprout noodles

Another lovely balance of flavors and textures for a quick, no-nonsense, yet healthy, tasty supper. If you want to be extravagant, use tiger shrimp or jumbo shrimp—I've even thrown in some baby scallops on occasion—and a selection of wild mushrooms.

Preparation: 10 minutes • Cooking time: 10 minutes • Serves 2

2 cups (175 g) medium egg noodles
2 teaspoons vegetable oil
1 garlic clove, chopped, or
 1 teaspoon garlic purée
1 tablespoon chopped cilantro
 or parsley
6 scallions, trimmed and
 diagonally sliced
1 red hot pepper, seeded and
 chopped
½ cup (100 g) mushrooms (oyster,

chestnut, or button), sliced
4 oz (100 g) cooked, peeled shrimp
 (about 10 medium)
3 tablespoons oyster sauce
1 tablespoon fresh lime juice
2 teaspoons sugar
1 cup (100 g) bean sprouts
cilantro or parsley sprigs, to garnish
 (optional)

1 Cook the noodles in boiling water for 4 minutes, or according to package instructions, then drain well.

2 Meanwhile, heat the oil in a frying pan and stir-fry the garlic, chopped cilantro or parsley, scallions, and hot pepper for 1 minute. Add the mushrooms and shrimp and stir-fry 1 minute more.

3 Stir in ½ cup (120 ml) of water, the oyster sauce, lime juice, and sugar. Cook briefly to heat through and reduce slightly. Stir in the noodles and bean sprouts and heat through. Toss well and garnish with cilantro or parsley, if liked. Serve immediately.

Roasted lemon bay-scented cod

Lemon and bay are wonderful ingredients to use when cooking fish, as the fragrance seeps into the fish. For a tasty addition to this aromatic dish, why not roast four stems of baby tomatoes on the vine with the fish, to serve as a colorful accompaniment?

Nutrition notes per serving:
- ★ calories 155
- ★ protein 28 g
- ★ carbohydrate 2 g
- ★ fat 4 g
- ★ saturated fat 1 g
- ★ fiber none
- ★ added sugar none
- ★ salt 0.48 g

Preparation: 10 minutes + 10 minutes standing time
• Cooking time: 10 minutes • Serves 4

4 garlic cloves, crushed
1 tablespoon chopped fresh parsley
1 tablespoon olive oil
1¼ lbs (600 g) cod fillets

2 lemons, thinly sliced
10 fresh bay leaves
salt and freshly ground black pepper

1 Preheat the oven to 425°F/220°C. Mix together the garlic, parsley, oil, and some salt and pepper. Rub the mixture over the fish fillets and set aside for 10 minutes or so.

2 Arrange the lemon slices and bay leaves on a baking sheet and place the cod fillets   on top. Cook in the oven for 8–10 minutes until just cooked and a little charred. Serve immediately.

Classic moules marinière

Nutrition notes
per serving:

★ calories 217
★ protein 20 g
★ carbohydrate 8 g
★ fat 10 g
★ saturated fat 7 g
★ fiber 1 g
★ added sugar none
★ salt 1.64 g

This French classic is really easy to make, and when mussels are in season—September to April—they're cheap and plentiful. They're always low in fat! To reduce the fat content even more for this dish, simply leave out the crème fraîche: The pan juices will still be dee-lish.

Preparation: 10 minutes • Cooking time: 15 minutes • Serves 4

2 tablespoons (25 g) butter
1 onion, chopped
2 garlic cloves, finely chopped
⅔ cup (150 ml) dry white wine
4½ lb (2 kg) live, clean mussels

⅔ cup (150 ml) fish stock
3 tablespoons reduced-fat crème fraîche or light cream
2 tablespoons chopped fresh parsley
salt and freshly ground black pepper

1   Melt the butter in a large pan and cook the onion and garlic over medium-low heat for 3–4 minutes until softened and lightly golden. Then pour in the wine, turn up the heat, and bring to a steaming boil. Now add the mussels.

2   Cover and cook over high heat for 4–5 minutes until all the shells have opened—give the pan a good shake halfway through the cooking time, holding the lid firmly in place. Transfer the mussels to a serving dish, discarding any that remain closed. Leave the juices behind in the saucepan.

3   Add the fish stock to the juices, bring to a boil, then reduce the heat. Stir the reduced-fat crème fraîche and parsley into the pan juices, add pepper, and check for salt. Ladle the pan juices over the mussels and serve hot.

Glazed monkfish skewers
with udon noodles

Nutrition notes
per serving:

★ calories 352
★ protein 28 g
★ carbohydrate 52 g
★ fat 5 g
★ saturated fat none
★ fiber 2 g
★ added sugar 3 g
★ salt 1.56 g

Thick Japanese rice noodles are a satisfying accompaniment to these succulent monkfish skewers. This dish is perfect for cooking on a grill, but if you do, remember that fish does tend to fall apart during cooking, so it is a good idea to buy a hinged grill basket for easy turning.

Preparation: 15 minutes • Cooking time: 10 minutes • Serves 4

18 oz (500 g) cubed monkfish, or
  any firm white fish
2 tablespoons soy sauce
1 tablespoon tomato purée
juice of 1 lime
1 tablespoon vinegar
1 tablespoon honey

½ teaspoon Thai fish sauce
  (nam pla)
½ teaspoon hot pepper oil
1 tablespoon chopped cilantro
9 oz (250 g) udon noodles
4 heads bok choy, roughly chopped

1 Thread the monkfish onto 8 skewers. If you use wooden skewers, you'll need to soak them for 20 minutes before you use them.

2 Mix together the soy sauce, tomato purée, lime juice, vinegar, honey, fish sauce, hot pepper oil, and cilantro, then brush over the kebabs.

3 Cook the skewers over hot coals or under a preheated hot broiler for about 6–8 minutes, turning frequently, until the fish is cooked through and a little charred.

4 Meanwhile, run the noodles under hot water to separate a little, then steam over a pan of boiling water with the bok choy for 3–4 minutes. Serve the monkfish skewers on top of the udon noodles.

Baked Cantonese cod corners

Nutrition notes
per serving:

★ calories 139
★ protein 28 g
★ carbohydrate 2 g
★ fat 2 g
★ saturated fat none
★ fiber none
★ added sugar none
★ salt 1.59 g

I use heavy-duty foil to make a tent in which the cod can steam in its own juices—it gives a very delicate, fragrant result. The real beauty of this dish is the delightful aroma that fills the air and your nostrils when you pop open the corner.

Preparation: 10 minutes • Cooking time: 8 minutes • Serves 4

1¼ lb (600 g) cod fillets
4-inch (10-cm) piece fresh ginger,
  peeled and cut into matchsticks
6 scallions, shredded
2 garlic cloves, finely chopped
2 tablespoons soy sauce

1 tablespoon wine vinegar
1 teaspoon sesame oil
1 teaspoon red pepper flakes
  (optional)
chopped cilantro, to serve

1 If you're not using a grill, preheat the oven to 400°F/200°C. Arrange each cod fillet in the center of its own large square of foil. Scatter over the ginger, scallions, and garlic. Drizzle each piece of fish with a little soy sauce, vinegar, and sesame oil, and sprinkle with a few red pepper flakes, if using. Pull the corners of the foil together and fold over the edges to make a tent around each fillet.

2 Grill over medium-hot coals for 8 minutes until the fish is just cooked. Or, if you don't have an outdoor grill, place the fish bundles on a baking sheet and bake in the oven for 20 minutes. Serve the bundles whole so as to capture that aromatic moment when you open them; alternatively, remove the fish from the parcels and transfer onto warmed serving plates. Serve with rice sprinkled with chopped cilantro.

Light and crunchy fish cakes

These oven-baked fish cakes are wonderful served with my Roasted Onion, Arugula, and Pecorino Salad (page 142). Why not make double the quantity and freeze half at the end of step 3 for a later date? You could also make the cakes using smoked cod or a combination of smoked cod and haddock.

Nutrition notes
per serving:

★ calories 316
★ protein 26 g
★ carbohydrate 43 g
★ fat 5 g
★ saturated fat 1 g
★ fiber 2 g
★ added sugar none
★ salt 2.56 g

Preparation: 25 minutes • Cooking time: 35–40 minutes • Serves 4

1 lb (450 g) baking potatoes, cubed (about 2 large)
12 oz (350 g) smoked haddock
1 hard-boiled egg
2 tablespoons snipped chives or chopped fresh parsley

2 tablespoons flour, seasoned with salt and pepper
1 egg, beaten
1 cup (100 g) white breadcrumbs
oil, for spraying
salt and freshly ground black pepper

1 Preheat the oven to 400°F/200°C. Cook the potatoes in a pan of boiling, salted water until tender. Drain and mash well.

2 Meanwhile, place the fish in a sauté pan and cover with boiling water. Bring to a boil and simmer for 5 minutes, until just cooked.

3 Drain the fish and remove the skin. Using a fork, flake the fish, discarding any bones. Mix together the potatoes, fish, hard-boiled egg, chives or parsley, and salt and pepper. Dust your hands with flour to shape the mixture into 4 or 8 even-sized round or triangular cakes.

4 Dust the fish cakes with the seasoned flour, dip in the beaten egg, then coat in the breadcrumbs, making sure the cakes are completely covered.

5 Spray a little oil onto a baking sheet and arrange the fish cakes on top. Spray with a little more oil and bake for 25–30 minutes until crisp and golden. Serve warm.

Cod kebab zingers with salsa tagliatelle

Nutrition notes
per serving:

★ calories 477
★ protein 38 g
★ carbohydrate 62 g
★ fat 10 g
★ saturated fat 1 g
★ fiber 4 g
★ added sugar none
★ salt 0.69 g

My lively lime marinade firms up the fish nicely, keeping it on the skewers rather than in the bottom of the grill pan once it's cooked. To add a kick to your pasta, add one small, fresh, seeded, chopped pepper—remember some are hot and some are not, so check out the hotness of the pepper before using.

Preparation: 15 minutes • Cooking time: 15 minutes • Serves 3

1 lb (450 g) skinned thick cod fillets,
  cubed
grated zest of 1 lime
juice of 2 limes
2 tablespoons olive oil
1½ cups (225 g) tagliatelle
8 oz (225 g) thin green beans,
  trimmed

½ pint (200 g) cherry tomatoes,
  halved
1 small red onion, finely chopped
1 tablespoon chopped fresh parsley
  or cilantro
salt and freshly ground black pepper

1 Mix together the cubed cod, lime zest, half the lime juice, and 1 tablespooon of the oil. Season with salt and pepper and set aside to marinate for 5 minutes.

2 Preheat the broiler to high. Thread the cod cubes onto 6 skewers, season, and broil for 8–10 minutes, turning once, until tender and golden.

3 Meanwhile, cook the tagliatelle in a large pan of boiling, salted water, according to package instructions, adding the green beans 3 minutes before the end of the cooking time. Drain. Heat the remaining oil in the pan and sauté the tomatoes and red onion for 2 minutes. Toss in the pasta and green beans, parsley or cilantro, and remaining lime juice. Season to taste and serve immediately with the fish kebabs.

If using wooden or bamboo skewers, first soak them in warm water for 20 minutes to prevent them from burning.

Seared squid with citrus mango salad

Nutrition notes
per serving:

★ calories 173
★ protein 16 g
★ carbohydrate 15 g
★ fat 6 g
★ saturated fat 1 g
★ fiber 2 g
★ added sugar none
★ salt 1.19 g

The secret of tasty, tender squid is not to overcook it. Once it turns from opaque to white and starts to curl up—hey presto!—it's cooked. It's best to get your grill pan, or frying pan, really hot before you start to sear the squid or, if you're in an al fresco mood, sear it over hot coals.

Preparation: 10 minutes • Cooking time: 4 minutes • Serves 4

2 tablespoons chopped cilantro
1 teaspoon Thai fish sauce (nam pla)
1 tablespoon soy sauce
juice of ½ lime
12 small squid tubes, thawed if
  frozen
1 tablespoon olive oil

1 small red onion, diced
mixed salad greens
1 ripe mango, skinned, pitted, and
  thinly sliced

1 Mix together the cilantro, fish sauce, soy sauce, and lime juice.

2 Slit the squid tubes down one side and open out flat. Score the inside flesh of the squid in a crisscross pattern.

3 Heat the oil on a grill pan or frying pan and stir-fry the squid and onion for 4–5 minutes (the squid will curl up and roll itself when cooked). Remove from the heat and pour over the cilantro mixture. Toss well to coat.

4 Arrange the salad greens and mango slices on individual serving plates, place the seared squid on top, and spoon over the remaining juices. Eat immediately.

Charred tuna with green lentil salad

Nutrition notes
per serving:

★ calories 404
★ protein 48 g
★ carbohydrate 30 g
★ fat 11 g
★ saturated fat 2 g
★ fiber 4 g
★ added sugar none
★ salt 2.97 g

Tuna is the filet mignon of the fish world. It should be cooked lightly, as overcooking will dry it out. For a great complementary flavor, use dried lentils cooked in chicken stock with a few vegetables (carrots, celery, onion, garlic) and a bay leaf.

Preparation: 15 minutes • Cooking time: 12 minutes • Serves 2

1¼ cups (150 g) dried green lentils, cooked
2 plum tomatoes, finely chopped
5 oz (50 g) mixed sweet pepper strips (red, green, or yellow)
1 hot pepper, seeded and finely chopped
1 scallion, trimmed and thinly sliced
2 tablespoons soy sauce

1 tablespoon white wine vinegar
1 tablespoon chopped mixed fresh herbs (e.g. cilantro, basil, and parsley)
2 small (5 oz, 150 g) fresh tuna steaks
2 teaspoons olive oil
salt and freshly ground black pepper
fresh basil leaves, to garnish

1 Put the cooked lentils in a pan and warm slightly. Remove from the heat and drain. (Remove cooking vegetables and bay leaf at this point.) Place in a large bowl, then add the chopped tomatoes, sweet pepper strips, hot pepper, and scallion. Now add the soy sauce, vinegar, and fresh herbs. Season and mix well. Set aside.

2 Heat a cast-iron ridged grill pan, or a frying pan, until hot. Season the tuna steaks and brush with the oil. Grill for 2–3 minutes on each side, depending on the thickness of the steaks. Place a mound of lentil salad in the middle of each plate, and arrange a tuna steak on top of the salad with a garnish of fresh basil leaves.

Lean and

Wok-it chicken chow mein

SOS chicken curry with
rice pilaf

Cajun chicken cutlets with
Spanish orange salad

Sticky garlic chicken skewers

Char-grilled pineapple
chicken pockets

Jamaican jerk chicken

Spicy chicken burgers

Crisp phyllo-wrapped
mustard chicken

Lemon garlic chicken
with coriander

luscious chicken

Charred chicken and
pepper fajitas

Oriental turkey with hot-wok
vegetables

Wok-it chicken chow mein

Nutrition notes
per serving:

★ calories 447
★ protein 35 g
★ carbohydrate 53 g
★ fat 11.8 g
★ saturated fat 1 g
★ fiber 5 g
★ added sugar 2 g
★ salt 2 g

For this quick noodle dish, shredded cooked chicken is stir-fried with garlic, ginger, soy sauce, and chili sauce and tossed with crunchy vegetables and tasty noodles—perfect for a quick supper. Why not try making this with different kinds of noodles, such as udon or rice noodles?

Preparation: 10 minutes • Cooking time: 15 minutes • Serves 3

2 cups (175 g) noodles
2 teaspoons sunflower oil
1 onion, thinly sliced
2 garlic cloves, thinly sliced
½-inch (1-cm) piece fresh ginger,
  peeled and finely chopped (optional)
1½ cups (175 g) bean sprouts

1 cup (175 g) snow peas, halved
  lengthwise, or peas
8 oz (225 g) lean cooked chicken,
  shredded (about 1 large breast)
2 tablespoons soy sauce
2 tablespoons sweet chili sauce
  (to make your own, see page 32)

1 Cook the noodles in a large pan of boiling, salted water according to the package instructions.

2 Meanwhile, heat the oil in a wok or large frying pan, and stir-fry the onion over high heat for 2–3 minutes until it begins to brown. Add the garlic, ginger (if using), bean sprouts, and snow peas or peas and stir-fry for 1 minute.

3 Drain the noodles well and add to the wok or frying pan, with the chicken and soy sauce; cook for 2 minutes until piping hot. Stir in the sweet chili sauce and serve immediately.

SOS chicken curry with rice pilaf

Nutrition notes
per serving:

★ calories 357
★ protein 25 g
★ carbohydrate 46.4 g
★ fat 9.4 g
★ saturated fat 2.4 g
★ fiber 1 g
★ added sugar 2 g
★ salt 1.74 g

If you have little time on your hands, but want a wonderful meal, and you don't mind using the occasional prepared ingredient, look no further—this dish is for you. Watch for reduced-fat pre-cooked chicken tikka breasts: they are much lower in fat than standard chicken tikka.

Preparation: 5 minutes • Cooking time: 15 minutes • Serves 6

500 g carton tomatoes in box
  (Pomi is one brand name)
1–2 tablespoons hot curry paste
1 lb (400 g) cooked boneless tandoori
  or tikka chicken breasts, cut into
  bite-sized pieces, or other Asian-
  style prepared chicken breasts
⅔ cup (150 ml) nonfat plain yogurt
½ teaspoon sugar

salt and freshly ground black pepper
For the rice
2 teaspoons vegetable oil
1 onion, sliced
3 cups (675 g) cooked white rice
1 teaspoon turmeric
1 oz (25 g) seedless raisins
chopped cilantro, to garnish
  (optional)

1 Place the tomatoes in a small pan, stir in the curry paste, and heat gently.

2 Meanwhile, for the rice, heat the oil in a wok and stir-fry the onion for
   4 minutes until nicely browned. Stir in the rice, turmeric, and raisins and heat
   gently for 3–4 minutes, adding a splash of water if the mixture is a little dry.

3 Add the chicken and yogurt to the tomato mixture, bring to a boil, and simmer
   for 2 minutes until warmed through. Stir in the sugar and season to taste.

4 Season the rice and divide between serving plates. Spoon over the chicken
   mixture and garnish with cilantro, if using.

Cajun chicken cutlets with Spanish orange salad

Nutrition notes
per serving:

★ calories 305
★ protein 40 g
★ carbohydrate 24 g
★ fat 6 g
★ saturated fat 1 g
★ fiber 3 g
★ added sugar none
★ salt 0.97 g

These Cajun-spiced chicken cutlets are served on top of a juicy, leafy salad—it's a sizzling combination! Look for chicken breast tenders (thinly sliced strips) in your local supermarket. They are ideal for this quick tasty recipe, but if you can't get hold of them, you can buy standard chicken breasts and slice them into thin strips yourself.

Preparation: 15 minutes • Cooking time: 25 minutes • Serves 4

For the Cajun chicken
12 skinless chicken breast tenders
juice of 1 lime
5 tablespoons flour
1 tablespoon Cajun seasoning
1 teaspoon cayenne pepper
½ teaspoon salt

For the salad
2 oranges
spinach and arugula greens
1 tablespoon olive oil
1 small red onion, thinly sliced

1 Preheat the oven to 425°F/220°C. Toss the chicken in the lime juice to coat. Place the flour, Cajun seasoning, cayenne pepper, and salt into a large bowl and mix well together.

2 Sprinkle the flour mixture onto a plate. Lift the chicken pieces out of the lime juice and press each side into the seasoned flour to coat evenly. Place the chicken on a wire rack and sit the rack on a baking sheet. Bake the chicken for 20–25 minutes.

3 While the chicken is cooking, peel the oranges, discarding the white pith. Cut into segments over a bowl to catch all the juice; this will make the basis of your dressing.

4 Toss the orange segments with the orange juice, salad greens, oil, and onion and divide between individual serving plates. Pile the crispy Cajun chicken on top to serve.

Sticky garlic chicken skewers

On a hot summer's day there's nothing better than these spicy chicken skewers sizzling away on the grill. Make the marinade the night before, add the chicken, and let stand overnight—it'll leave you time to relax with your guests. If the weather's not on your side, simply cook under the broiler.

Preparation: 5 minutes + marinating time • Cooking time: 10 minutes • Serves 4

3 garlic cloves, crushed
2 tablespoons honey
4 tablespoons tomato ketchup
4 tablespoons Worcestershire sauce
2 teaspoons English or dijon mustard

2 teaspoons Tabasco sauce
3 skinless, boneless chicken breasts,
 cut into thin strips
salt and freshly ground black pepper
salad and new potatoes, to serve

1 Soak twelve 10-inch (25-cm) bamboo skewers in water for at least 20 minutes.

2 Meanwhile, mix together the garlic, honey, ketchup, Worcestershire sauce, mustard, and Tabasco, and season with salt and freshly ground black pepper. Toss in the chicken and stir until well combined, transfer to a nonmetallic dish, cover, and marinate for 20–30 minutes or overnight.

3 Preheat the broiler to high. Thread the marinated chicken onto the skewers. Arrange on a foil-lined baking sheet and broil for 6–7 minutes, turning occasionally until well browned and cooked through. Or cook over the hot coals of an outdoor grill for 5–6 minutes. Serve with mixed salad and baby new potatoes.

Char-grilled pineapple chicken pockets

Nutrition notes per serving:

★ calories 199
★ protein 34 g
★ carbohydrate 13 g
★ fat 2 g
★ saturated fat 1 g
★ fiber none
★ added sugar 9 g
★ salt 0.23 g

Now here's a delicious low-fat fruity chicken feast. When you combine foods and they work well together, the finished dish can be a real delight. Chicken and pineapple work beautifully together, especially with the added flavor of scallion.

Preparation: 20 minutes • Cooking time: 20 minutes • Serves 6

6 large skinless, boneless chicken breasts
1 cup (225 g) prepared fresh pineapple or canned pineapple in natural juice
2–3 scallions, trimmed and thinly sliced

4 tablespoons (50 g) caster sugar
pinch cayenne powder or red pepper flakes
salt and freshly ground black pepper

1 Preheat the broiler to medium. Cut a small shallow pocket into the side of the thickest part of each chicken breast.

2 Drain the pineapple and reserve the juice. Finely chop the pineapple (or run it through a food processor) and mix with the scallions, a little salt, and pepper. Spoon the mixture into each pocket, but do not overfill the pocket as you need to be able to secure it with a short, thin metal skewer or a long toothpick. If using toothpicks, first soak them in water for 20 minutes.

3 Mix the reserved pineapple juice and sugar together in a small pan and stir over low heat until the sugar has dissolved. Bring the mixture to a boil and boil vigorously until it is syrupy and reduced to about 4 tablespoons. Stir in the cayenne powder or red pepper flakes.

4 Broil the chicken for about 10 minutes, turning now and then until it is about half cooked. Then brush over some of the pineapple glaze and continue to cook for another 10 minutes, turning and brushing the chicken with more glaze until it is cooked through. Serve with baked sweet potatoes.

Nutrition notes
per serving:

★ calories 190
★ protein 36 g
★ carbohydrate 8 g
★ fat 2 g
★ saturated fat 1 g
★ fiber 1 g
★ added sugar none
★ salt 4 g

Jamaican jerk chicken

This classic Jamaican jerk chicken is the perfect way to enjoy chicken without adding lots of fat. Be careful with the habañeros or Scotch bonnet peppers that are used in the marinade, as they are extremely hot—some say the hottest in the world. Don't tell my dad; he eats them for breakfast!

Preparation: 10 minutes + 12–24 hours marinating time
• Cooking time: 30 minutes • Serves 6

2 medium (225 g) onions, quartered
2 habañeros or Scotch bonnet peppers, halved and seeded
2-inch (5-cm) piece fresh ginger, peeled and roughly chopped
½ teaspoon ground allspice
leaves from 2 long, fresh thyme sprigs
1 teaspoon freshly ground black pepper
½ cup (120 ml) white wine vinegar
½ cup (120 ml) dark soy sauce
6 large skinless chicken pieces
rice, hot peppers, and shredded scallions, to serve

1 Put all the ingredients, except for the chicken, into a food processor and whizz until smooth.

2 Put the chicken in a large, shallow nonmetallic dish, pour over the sauce, cover with plastic wrap, and marinate in the refrigerator for 24 hours, turning the chicken every now and then. If you don't have time to marinate overnight, cut some deep grooves into the chicken to allow the spices to penetrate the chicken more quickly, and marinate for a few hours before cooking.

3 Preheat the broiler to medium. Grill the chicken for 25–30 minutes—or grill over medium coals—basting now and then with the leftover sauce. Alternatively, you can bake the chicken pieces on a baking tray in a medium-hot oven (400°F/200°C) for 25–30 minutes. As the chicken cooks, the thickened sauce will blacken in places, but as it falls off it will leave behind tender, moist jerk meat underneath. Serve with rice, hot peppers, and shredded scallions for the perfect flavor combination.

Spicy chicken burgers

really low fat!

Nutrition notes per serving:

★ calories 149
★ protein 28 g
★ carbohydrate 1 g
★ fat 3 g
★ saturated fat 1 g
★ fiber none
★ added sugar none
★ salt 0.58 g

Ground chicken is readily available in grocery stores now. Try ground turkey, too—it's really lean and low in fat. Just because it's a healthy option doesn't mean the burger has to be small. This burger is big on size, style, and, of course, taste.

Preparation: 10 minutes • Cooking time: 10 minutes • Serves 4

18 oz (500 g) lean minced chicken
2 garlic cloves, crushed
1 red hot pepper, seeded and finely chopped
1 tablespoon chopped fresh mint
2 tablespoons chopped fresh parsley or cilantro

2 teaspoons Worcestershire sauce
olive oil, for brushing
salt and freshly ground black pepper
To serve
hamburger buns
arugula and tomato slices

1 Mix together the ground chicken, garlic, hot pepper, herbs, Worcestershire sauce, and plenty of salt and pepper.

2 Shape the mixture into 4 even-sized burgers, then brush lightly with the oil. Preheat the broiler to medium.

3 Broil for 5 minutes on each side—or cook on a medium-hot barbecue—until well browned and cooked through. Serve in hamburger buns with arugula and juicy sliced tomatoes.

Crisp phyllo-wrapped mustard chicken

Crisp phyllo pastry surrounds this aromatic chicken, sealing in those lovely flavors. A great low-fat dish for entertaining served with broccoli raab. Traditionally, melted butter is spread between the layers of phyllo, but by using oil from a sprayer, you can make this dish with less than half the fat.

Preparation: 25 minutes • Cooking time: 30 minutes • Serves 4

2 teaspoons olive oil
1 lb (500 g) skinless, boneless cooked chicken breasts (4 small breasts)
2 teaspoons fresh marjoram leaves, finely chopped
1 tablespoon Dijon mustard

2 garlic cloves, crushed
finely grated zest of 1 lemon
8 sheets phyllo dough
salt and freshly ground black pepper
oil, for spraying
broccoli raab (optional)

1 Heat the oil in a large frying pan and sauté the chicken for 4 minutes on each side until lightly golden.

2 Mix together the marjoram, mustard, garlic, and lemon zest; season generously. Spread the mustard mixture evenly over each chicken breast.

3 Preheat the oven to 375°F/190°C. Lay a sheet of phyllo dough flat on a work surface and spray with a little oil, then top with another sheet of phyllo. Lay 1 chicken breast in the center of the dough, lift the edges of the dough over the chicken, and scrunch over the top to enclose. Repeat with the remaining phyllo dough and mustard chicken breasts to make 4 bundles. Arrange on a baking sheet and bake for 20 minutes until crunchy and golden.

4 Place the phyllo-wrapped chicken bundles onto warmed serving plates and serve with fresh, steamed broccoli raab.

really low fat!

Lemon garlic chicken with coriander

Nutrition notes
per serving:

★ calories 195
★ protein 32 g
★ carbohydrate 14 g
★ fat 2 g
★ saturated fat none
★ fiber none
★ added sugar 11 g
★ salt 0.22 g

Lemon chicken is one of my favorite dishes—the acid from the lemon juice makes a wonderful marinade and helps make the chicken beautifully tender. I sometimes roast some extra lemon wedges in with the chicken and serve them as a garnish. It's especially good served with Spicy Casablanca Couscous (see page 163).

Preparation: 10 minutes + marinating time • Cooking time: 40 minutes • Serves 4

4 skinless, boneless chicken breasts
3 garlic cloves, crushed
finely grated zest and juice of
  3 lemons
1 red hot pepper, seeded and finely
  chopped

4 tablespoons honey
2 tablespoons ground coriander
salt and freshly ground black pepper
small handful of cilantro, lemon
  wedges, and roasted vine
  tomatoes, to serve

1 Season the chicken. Mix together the garlic, lemon zest and juice, hot pepper, honey, and ground coriander. Turn the chicken in the marinade to coat and then marinate in a covered, nonmetallic dish for 2–3 hours or overnight in the refrigerator.

2 Preheat the oven to 400°F/200°C. Roast the chicken in the marinade for 35–40 minutes until the chicken is tender.

3 Place the chicken breasts onto warmed serving plates and garnish with sprigs of cilantro and roast lemon wedges. Serve with roasted tomatoes on the vine and some of my Spicy Casablanca Couscous.

Charred chicken and pepper fajitas

Nutrition notes
per serving:

★ calories 544
★ protein 49 g
★ carbohydrate 66 g
★ fat 11 g
★ saturated fat 4 g
★ fiber 4 g
★ added sugar none
★ salt 1.3 g

The sight and sound of sizzling chicken and vegetables arriving at your table is a joy, and it doesn't have to be limited to a restaurant; this dish can be made at home with surprisingly little effort. It's so simple that once you've tried it, it's sure to be a favorite.

Preparation: 15 minutes • Cooking time: 10 minutes • Serves 2

2 large skinless, boneless chicken breasts, cut into ½-inch (1-cm) wide strips
1 sweet yellow pepper, cut lengthwise into ½-inch (1-cm) wide strips
1 sweet red pepper, cut lengthwise into ½-inch (1-cm) wide strips
1 red onion, thickly sliced
½ teaspoon dried oregano
¼ teaspoon crushed hot peppers
1 tablespoon vegetable oil
grated zest and juice of 1 lime, plus an extra lime for serving
4 x 8-inch (20-cm) flour tortillas
leafy salad
8 oz (150 ml) carton nonfat plain yogurt
salt and freshly ground black pepper

1 Place the chicken strips, sweet peppers, onion, oregano, hot pepper, vegetable oil, and lime zest and juice in a large bowl. Add plenty of seasoning and toss together until well mixed.

2 Heat a flat griddle pan or heavy, nonstick frying pan. Add the chicken mixture and cook over high heat for 6–8 minutes, turning once or twice until the mixture is well browned, lightly charred, and cooked through.

3 Warm the tortillas in the microwave or in a dry frying pan for a few seconds.

4 Serve separately, or pile the chicken mixture in the middle of your warm tortillas, add salad, a squeeze of lime, and a dollop of the yogurt, roll up, and enjoy.

Oriental turkey with hot-wok vegetables

Nutrition notes
per serving:

★ calories 208
★ protein 39 g
★ carbohydrate 3 g
★ fat 4 g
★ saturated fat 1 g
★ fiber none
★ added sugar 1 g
★ salt 2.02 g

Turkey meat is not only economical, it is very lean and therefore low in fat. Here it is marinated and served in a quick Oriental-style stir-fry. If you want a change, why not try this recipe with chicken breast or lean pork loin? I've even made it with firm fish fillets.

Preparation: 10 minutes plus marinating time • Cooking time: 6–8 minutes • Serves 4

2 tablespoons dry sherry
1 tablespoon sweet chili sauce (to make your own, see page 32)
2 tablespoons dark soy sauce
1 teaspoon sesame oil
1-inch (2.5-cm) piece fresh ginger, peeled and shredded
4 turkey cutlets (about 5 oz/150 g each)

2 teaspoons sunflower oil
1 red hot pepper, seeded and thinly sliced
1 cup (225 g) shiitake mushrooms, halved
6 scallions, trimmed and thinly sliced
4 large heads bok choy, trimmed and separated into individual leaves

1 Mix together the sherry, chili sauce, soy sauce, sesame oil, and ginger in a large, shallow, nonmetallic dish. Coat the turkey cutlets in the marinade. Cover and marinate for at least 30 minutes, or overnight if you have time.

2 Preheat a large ridged griddle pan or a frying pan until smoking. Remove the turkey from the marinade, lay across the ridges of the griddle pan, and sear for 2–3 minutes on each side.

3 Meanwhile, heat the sunflower oil in a large wok or frying pan and stir-fry the hot pepper and mushrooms for 2 minutes. Pour over the marinade and bring to a boil. Stir in the scallions and bok choy and stir-fry for 1–2 minutes, until the vegetables are just wilted and the sauce has thickened. Serve immediately with the seared turkey cutlets.

Quick

Grilled Cajun steak with
charred tomato salad

Low-fat cassoulet in a hurry

Moroccan-style lamb kebabs

meaty main dishes

Thai-style ground meat with
fragrant rice

Peri peri pork medallions
and lemon

Scalloped potato
shepherd's pie

Café chili beef tacos

Spiced Matzalán meatballs

Harissa lamb with
low-fat hummus

Lean smoked-ham paella

Grilled Cajun steak with charred tomato salad

Nutrition notes
per serving:

★ calories 291
★ protein 38 g
★ carbohydrate 11 g
★ fat 11 g
★ saturated fat 3 g
★ fiber 2 g
★ added sugar none
★ salt 1.81 g

Sirloin is very lean beef, but there is fat around the top edge of each steak and marbled throughout the meat itself. You can trim off the fat around the edge to , but the marbled fat gives the meat succulence and flavor. The leanest cuts are labeled "loin" or "round," as in "sirloin round."

Preparation: 15 minutes + standing time • Cooking time: 15 minutes
•Serves 2

grated zest of 1 lemon
2 garlic cloves
½ teaspoon black peppercorns
½ teaspoon cumin seeds
1 teaspoon dried oregano
½ teaspoon cayenne pepper
½ teaspoon coarse sea salt
2 x 5 oz (150 g) lean sirloin steaks

For the charred tomato salad
3 large plum tomatoes
1 small bunch cilantro
1 small bunch fresh mint
1 red onion, finely chopped
1 green hot pepper, finely chopped
2 teaspoons olive oil
juice of ½ lemon
salt and freshly ground black pepper
leafy salad, to serve

1 Using a mortar and pestle, a mini food processor, or a coffee grinder, grind the lemon zest, garlic, peppercorns, and cumin seeds together until well blended. Add the oregano, cayenne, and salt, and grind again.

2 Rub the mixture into the meat and set aside for an hour or two. Meanwhile, halve the tomatoes lengthwise and place on the grill or a hot, ridged griddle pan, or a frying pan, cut sides down, for 5–8 minutes, until softened and a little charred.

3 Finely chop the herbs and mix with the tomatoes, onion, hot pepper, oil, and lemon juice; season well to taste.

4 Grill the steaks or cook on the hot, ridged griddle pan or frying pan for 3–4 minutes on each side. Serve with the charred tomatoes and leafy green salad. Wow!

Low-fat cassoulet in a hurry

Nutrition notes
per serving:

★ calories 338
★ protein 33 g
★ carbohydrate 21 g
★ fat 11 g
★ saturated fat 4 g
★ fiber 6 g
★ added sugar none
★ salt 1.62 g

Cassoulet is a wonderful hearty dish from the Languedoc region of France. Meat and beans are cooked with spices until tender, and the dish is topped off with crunchy bread-crumbs. Like paella, cassoulet can be made in many different styles. Goose or duck confits and sausages with bacon or salt pork are all delicious, but my version is tasty *and* low in fat.

Preparation: 10 minutes • Cooking time: 40 minutes • Serves 4

1 tablespoon olive oil
1 onion, chopped
2 garlic cloves, finely chopped
8 oz (250 g) cubed lamb or pork
15 oz (400 g) can chopped tomatoes
2 carrots, diced
⅔ cup (150 ml) red wine
⅔ cup (150 ml) lamb stock
1 teaspoon each fresh, or ¼
  teaspoon each dried, rosemary,
  thyme, and parsley

15 oz (400 g) can haricot or white
  beans, drained
2 tablespoons fresh white
  breadcrumbs
salt and freshly ground black pepper
chopped fresh parsley, to garnish
thin green beans, to serve

1 Heat the oil in a large pan and cook the onion and garlic for 3–4 minutes until softened. Add the lamb or pork and stir-fry for 5 minutes.

2 Stir in the tomatoes, carrots, wine, stock, and herbs, then cover and cook over medium heat for 20–25 minutes until the meat is tender.

3 Preheat the broiler to high. Stir the beans into the pan, season with salt and pepper, and transfer to a heatproof serving dish. Sprinkle with breadcrumbs, then broil for a few minutes until the topping is golden. Serve with thin green beans and a nice fruity red wine.

Moroccan-style lamb kebabs

These kebabs are a great way to cook meat without adding any fat. Why not roast some pumpkin wedges rubbed with a touch of grain mustard and a splash of lemon juice to serve with them? Harissa is a fiery red hot-pepper paste from Africa; it can be found in supermarkets or your local specialty store.

Preparation: 20 minutes + marinating time • Cooking time: 15 minutes • Serves 4

18 oz (500 g) boned shoulder or
  leg of lamb
1 teaspoon olive oil
2 tablespoons lemon juice
1 teaspoon ground cumin
1 teaspoon ground coriander
½ teaspoon ground turmeric

½ tablespoon paprika
1 garlic clove, crushed
1 tablespoon harissa
1 small red onion, unpeeled
1 small lemon
salt and freshly ground black pepper
cilantro, to serve

1 If you're not using an outdoor grill, preheat the broiler to high. Trim any excess fat off the outside of the lamb and then cut into 2-inch (5-cm) chunks. Place in a nonmetallic bowl with the oil, lemon juice, spices, garlic, harissa, and some seasoning and mix well. Cover and marinate at room temperature for 2 hours, or overnight in the refrigerator.

2 Peel the onion, leaving the root end intact, and then cut into 8 wedges so that the slices of onion stay together at the root of each wedge. Cut the lemon into 8 wedges.

3 Thread the lamb chunks and lemon and onion wedges alternately onto skewers—you will need four 12-inch (30-cm) flat metal ones—and place under a preheated hot broiler, or over medium-hot coals, for 10–15 minutes. Turn now and then until the lamb is nicely browned on the outside, but still pink in the center. Serve with cilantro and roasted pumpkin wedges, if liked.

Thai-style ground meat with fragrant rice

Nutrition notes
per serving:

★ calories 413
★ protein 31 g
★ carbohydrate 63 g
★ fat 6 g
★ saturated fat 1 g
★ fiber 1 g
★ added sugar none
★ salt 1.98 g

There are so many exciting flavors associated with Thai food. Here I've taken a classic Bolognese sauce and added some of those flavors to create something really special—and it's low in fat, too. If you're a vegetarian you don't have to miss out; simply substitute Quorn for the meat.

Preparation: 10 minutes • Cooking time: 20 minutes • Serves 4

2 cups (250 g) long-grain or Thai
 fragrant rice
1 tablespoon vegetable oil
1 onion, halved and sliced
1 garlic clove, chopped
1 red pepper, cored, seeded and
 roughly chopped
1 lb (450 g) ground turkey or pork

½ teaspoon cayenne powder
¾ cup (175 ml) chicken stock
2 teaspoons cornstarch
2 tablespoons dark soy sauce
handful of fresh basil leaves, plus
 extra to garnish
salt and freshly ground black pepper

1 Cook the rice until tender, following package directions.

2 Meanwhile, heat the oil in a pan and cook the onion for 3–4 minutes until golden. Stir in the garlic and red pepper and cook for 4 minutes, then add the ground meat and cayenne powder and cook for 2–3 minutes until well browned. Stir in the stock, bring to a boil, and simmer for 5 minutes.

3 Blend the cornstarch with 1 tablespoon of water and the soy sauce until smooth, add to the pan, and stir until slightly thickened; season and stir in the basil leaves. Spoon the cooked rice into bowls, top with the Thai ground meat, and serve with a scattering of fresh basil leaves.

Peri peri pork medallions
and lemon

Peri peri sauce is a fiery Portuguese condiment that is also popular in Brazil and parts of Africa. It is sometimes known as piri piri or pili pili and is often served with chicken or fish, though I like it best with pork. Peri peri sauce is now available in specialty food stores.

Preparation: 10 minutes • Cooking time: 6 minutes • Serves 4

2 lemons
vegetable oil, for brushing

18 oz (500 g) lean pork tenderloin
6 tablespoons peri peri sauce

1 Very thinly slice the lemons and brush lightly with oil. Cut the pork loin into rounds ½ inch (1 cm) thick and brush with 1 tablespoon of the peri peri sauce.

2 Place a lemon slice on top of each piece of pork and pin in place with a long toothpick. You will need to soak the sticks for 20 minutes before using them. Cook over hot coals, lemon-sides down first, for 2–3 minutes on each side, until well browned and cooked through—the lemons should look a little charred. If you don't have a grill, cook under a preheated broiler for 4–5 minutes on each side.

3 Arrange on a serving platter with a little bowl of the remaining sauce for drizzling over. Serve with stir-fried mixed vegetables.

Scalloped potato shepherd's pie

Nutrition notes per serving:

★ calories 343
★ protein 28 g
★ carbohydrate 35 g
★ fat 11 g
★ saturated fat 4 g
★ fiber 5 g
★ added sugar none
★ salt 2.09 g

You really can't beat an old classic. To make it a bit different, I've added soy sauce and Tabasco to the lean ground meat for a real kick. I've also borrowed the topping from a traditional Lancashire hotpot—layers of sliced potato cooked until crispy and golden.

Preparation: 15 minutes • Cooking time: 35 minutes • Serves 4

1 lb (450 g) baking potatoes, thinly sliced (about 2 large)
1 teaspoon vegetable oil
2 carrots, diced
1 onion, finely chopped
1 lb (450 g) lean ground lamb
1¼ cups (300 ml) hot lamb stock
1 tablespoon brown sauce
2 tablespoons soy sauce

1 tablespoon cornstarch
½ cup (100 g) frozen peas
few drops Tabasco
3 tomatoes, thinly sliced
4 tablespoons (50 g) finely grated reduced-fat Cheddar cheese, (optional, but nice)
salt and freshly ground black pepper

1 Cook the potatoes in a large pan of boiling, salted water for 3–4 minutes. Drain well.

2 Preheat the oven to 400°F/200°C. Meanwhile, heat the oil in a large frying pan and cook the carrot and onion for about 1 minute over medium-high heat, then add the ground lamb and stir-fry until well browned. Pour in the hot stock and stir in the brown sauce and soy sauce. Bring to a boil and simmer rapidly for 3–4 minutes.

3 Mix the cornstarch and a little water to a paste, and stir into the lamb mixture with the peas; bring back to a boil, stirring, until slightly thickened. Season with salt, pepper, and Tabasco, to taste.

5 Spoon the ground-lamb mixture into a heatproof dish and top with overlapping slices of potato and tomato to cover the ground-lamb mixture completely. Sprinkle with grated cheese, if using. Bake for 25 minutes, until golden.

Café chili beef tacos

Nutrition notes
per serving:

★ calories 264
★ protein 23 g
★ carbohydrate 18 g
★ fat 11 g
★ saturated fat 4 g
★ fiber 4 g
★ added sugar none
★ salt 1.16 g

This is a fantastic chili with a really developed flavor, which it gets from my secret ingredient—coffee! Try it, it really packs a punch. Serve this chili in fluffy baked potatoes for a tasty alternative, or use it to fill soft flour tortillas if you can't get hold of taco shells.

Preparation: 10 minutes • Cooking time: 30 minutes • Serves 6

1 teaspoon vegetable oil
1 onion, finely chopped
2 garlic cloves, finely chopped
2 red hot peppers, seeded and finely chopped
l8 oz (500 g) lean minced beef
1 teaspoon Chinese five-spice powder
15 oz (400 g) can kidney beans, drained

15 oz (400 g) can chopped tomatoes
⅔ cup (150 ml) strong black coffee
salt and freshly ground black pepper
To serve
6 taco shells
shredded lettuce
reduced-fat sour cream (optional)
paprika

1 Heat the oil in a large pan and cook the onion, garlic, and hot peppers for 3–4 minutes, until beginning to soften. Add the ground beef and five-spice powder and cook for 3–4 minutes more, stirring, until the meat begins to brown.

2 Add the kidney beans, tomatoes, and coffee. Bring to a boil and simmer for 20 minutes, until the mixture is thick and fairly dark. Season to taste.

3 Fill the taco shells with shredded lettuce, then pile in the chili mixture. Top with a spoonful of sour cream, if liked, and a shake of paprika, and serve with a leafy green salad. A bottle of chilled Mexican beer is always a winner with this recipe!

Spiced Matzalán meatballs

Nutrition notes
per serving:

★ calories 220
★ protein 26 g
★ carbohydrate 4 g
★ fat 11 g
★ saturated fat 5 g
★ fiber none
★ added sugar none
★ salt 0.49 g

These delicious moist little meatballs, delicately flavored with spices from the Middle East, taste fabulous topped with yogurt and red onion. Serve them rolled up in soft, warm flat breads—you can also use flour tortillas. Fill them out with fresh salad ingredients for a complete meal.

Preparation: 15 minutes • Cooking time: 12 minutes • Serves 4

18 oz (500 g) lean minced lamb
pinch salt
1 onion, finely chopped
2 teaspoons ground cumin
1 teaspoon ground allspice
¼ teaspoon cayenne pepper
4 tablespoons roughly chopped
  cilantro

To serve
4 small Middle Eastern flat breads,
  i.e. pita
crisp lettuce leaves
1 red onion, thinly sliced
4 tablespoons nonfat plain yogurt
1 lemon, cut into 4 wedges

1 Place the lamb, salt, onion, cumin, allspice, cayenne, and cilantro in a food processor and work until well blended. Using wet hands, shape the mixture into 20 meatballs and cook over hot coals or in a nonstick frying pan for 10 minutes, turning frequently until well browned.

2 Warm the flat breads in the frying pan for 1–2 minutes on each side, until softened and warmed through.

3 Scatter lettuce leaves and the red onion over the flat breads. Arrange the meatballs on top and drizzle with a little yogurt. If you like, you can roll the flat breads up into a handheld snack. Serve with the lemon wedges.

Harissa lamb with low-fat hummus

Nutrition notes
per serving:

★ calories 295
★ protein 23 g
★ carbohydrate 27 g
★ fat 11 g
★ saturated fat 4 g
★ fiber 2 g
★ added sugar none
★ salt 1.61 g

The secret to char-grilling lamb is to cook it over high heat, searing in all the juices. Then just let it sit for a few minutes to relax, so that the meat becomes tender and wonderfully juicy. It's really not difficult, and I guarantee that these delicious lamb pitas are well worth the effort.

Preparation: 15 minutes + marinating time • Cooking time: 15 minutes
• Serves 4

1 tablespoon harissa or other chili
  paste or sauce
juice of 1 lemon
2 tablespoons chopped fresh mint
½ teaspoon sea salt

12 oz (350 g) lean lamb tenderloin
4 pita breads
bunch fresh arugula
4 tablespoons reduced-fat hummus
lemon wedges, to serve

1 Mix together the harissa or chili paste or sauce, lemon juice, chopped mint, and sea salt. Add the lamb tenderloin, turning to coat in the mixture, and set aside to marinate for 10 minutes or so.

2 Heat a grill pan or a frying pan, for 2–3 minutes until hot. Add the lamb tenderloin and cook for 8–12 minutes, until well browned but still a little pink in the center; remove from heat and allow to rest for 5 minutes to tenderize the meat. Warm the pitas in the same pan.

3 Cut the pitas in half and fill each pocket with arugula.

4 Diagonally slice the lamb into ½-inch (1-cm) thick slices and pack into the pitas. Top with a dollop of reduced-fat hummus and serve warm with lemon wedges for squeezing over.

Lean smoked-ham paella

Nutrition notes
per serving:
★ calories 363
★ protein 22 g
★ carbohydrate 53 g
★ fat 8 g
★ saturated fat 1 g
★ fiber 3 g
★ added sugar none
★ salt 2.52 g

Paella is a great dish to master: once you have the basics, you can make seemingly endless combinations of lean meat, fish, and vegetables. The paprika and turmeric give this dish its distinctive color and flavor. A complete meal in itself, it needs no accompaniment.

Preparation: 20 minutes • Cooking time: 25–30 minutes • Serves 4

2 tablespoons vegetable oil
1 onion, sliced
1 red sweet pepper cored, seeded, and sliced
1 garlic clove, crushed
1 cup (200 g) long-grain rice
6 oz (175 g) lean, smoked ham, roughly diced
4 cups (900 ml) chicken or vegetable stock

½ teaspoon each paprika and ground turmeric (or a few saffron strands, if you have them)
4 oz (100 g) shrimp, thawed if frozen (about 10 medium)
½ cup (100 g) frozen peas
salt and freshly ground black pepper

1 Heat the oil in a large frying pan and cook the onion for 3–4 minutes until softened and golden. Add the red sweet pepper, garlic, and rice and stir-fry for 1 minute. Add the ham, stock, paprika, and turmeric or saffron, bring to a boil and simmer for 12 minutes.

2 Stir in the shrimp and peas and cook for 3–4 minutes more, until the rice and vegetables are tender. Season to taste, then serve immediately.

Light and

Tomato, feta, and basil pizza

Black-eyed peas and
squash stew

Shiitake mushroom and
noodle-heaven stir-fry

Spicy beanburgers

Moroccan pumpkin and
potato stew

easy vegetarian

Oven-baked asparagus and
tomato risotto

Butternut squash and sweet
potato curry

Hot Mexican tamale
bean pie

Smoked eggplant and
vegetable curry

Pasta primavera with cherry
tomato sauce

Tomato, feta, and basil pizza

Nutrition notes
per serving:

★ calories 204
★ protein 9 g
★ carbohydrate 32 g
★ fat 6 g
★ saturated fat 3 g
★ fiber 4 g
★ added sugar none
★ salt 1.11 g

This pizza is quick and easy to make, ready for the kids to eat when they get home from school. For extra excitement, experiment with other low-fat toppings. Try parboiling zucchini slices and adding them along with some caramelized onions. Once cooked, scatter with fresh peppery arugula.

Preparation: 20 minutes • Cooking time: 20 minutes • Serves 4

1 package pizza-crust mix
2 tablespoons fresh mixed herbs
  (e.g., basil, rosemary, flat-leaf
  parsley), roughly chopped
2 ripe plum tomatoes, cut into
  wedges
8 cherry tomatoes, halved

8 firm vine-ripened tomatoes,
  cut into chunks
1 red onion, cut into thin wedges
6 tablespoons (75 g) crumbled
  feta cheese,
salt and freshly ground black pepper
fresh basil leaves, to garnish

1 Preheat the oven to 425°F/220°C. Preheat a large baking sheet in the oven at the same time.

2 Mix together the pizza-crust mix and the herbs. Follow the package directions to form a soft dough. Knead lightly on a floured surface until the dough is smooth. Roll out to about a 10-inch (25-cm) circle.

3 Lift the pizza circle onto the preheated baking sheet and scatter over the tomatoes, onion, and feta cheese. Season and bake for 20 minutes until golden. Scatter over the basil leaves to garnish.

Black-eyed peas
and squash stew

Nutrition notes
per serving:

★ calories 387
★ protein 14 g
★ carbohydrate 60 g
★ fat 11.5 g
★ saturated fat 1 g
★ fiber 10 g
★ added sugar none
★ salt 1.33 g

This hearty stew positively oozes goodness, yet it's easy to make and tastes terrific. The beauty of a one-pot meal is not just fewer dishes to wash, but also the fact that all the vitamins and minerals are kept in the sauce. This is the ideal comfort food.

Preparation: 20 minutes • Cooking time: 35 minutes • Serves 3

2 tablespoons olive oil
½ teaspoon cumin seeds
½ teaspoon mustard seeds
1 onion, chopped
1 garlic clove, finely chopped
1 red hot pepper, seeded and sliced
1 lb (450 g) potatoes, scrubbed and roughly chopped (about 2 large)
2 tablespoons curry paste or powder
2¼ cups (600 ml) vegetable stock

1 lb (450 g) butternut squash, pumpkin, or kabocha, peeled and roughly diced
15 oz (400 g) can black-eyed peas, drained
2 tomatoes, each cut into 6 wedges
salt and freshly ground black pepper
2 tablespoons chopped cilantro or parsley, to garnish (optional)
lemon wedges, to serve

1 Heat the oil in a large pan, add the cumin and mustard seeds, and cook for 1 minute. When they begin to splutter and pop, add the onion, garlic, and hot pepper and cook for 3–4 minutes until softened.

2 Stir in the potatoes and cook for 3 minutes. Add the curry paste and vegetable stock, bring to a boil and simmer for 5 minutes. Add the squash, butternut squash, pumpkin, or kabocha and simmer for 15 minutes more, until the vegetables are tender. Add the black-eyed peas and tomatoes and continue to cook for 2–3 minutes. Season to taste.

3 Divide the stew between individual dishes, sprinkle over the cilantro or parsley, and serve with the lemon wedges.

Shiitake mushroom and noodle-heaven stir-fry

Nutrition notes
per serving:

★ calories 430
★ protein 13 g
★ carbohydrate 74 g
★ fat 11 g
★ saturated fat 1 g
★ fiber 2 g
★ added sugar 8 g
★ salt 2.12 g

Look for black bean paste in Asian food stores. If you can't get hold of it, you can use black bean sauce instead. Bok choy is sold in large supermarkets and has a wonderful tender green leaf and a crisp crunchy stalk. Use baby spinach leaves or napa cabbage as an alternative.

Preparation: 10 minutes • Cooking time: 15 minutes • Serves 4

12 oz (325 g) medium egg noodles
2 teaspoons vegetable oil
1 red onion, thinly sliced
2 garlic cloves, crushed
2-inch (5-cm) piece fresh ginger,
  peeled and finely chopped
2 tablespoons black bean paste

2 teaspoons chili sauce
2 tablespoons light soy sauce
2 tablespoons sugar
1 large head bok choy, leaves
  separated
1 cup (250 g) shiitake mushrooms,
  sliced

1 Cook the noodles according to the package instructions. Drain.

2 Heat the oil in a wok until hot and smoking. Add the onion, garlic, and ginger and cook for 1 minute, stirring. Stir in the black bean paste, chili sauce, soy sauce, sugar, and 2 tablespoons of water. Bring to a boil, then toss in the noodles, making sure they are well coated in the sauce.

3 Now stir in the bok choy and mushrooms and stir-fry for 2–3 minutes until the bok choy is just beginning to wilt and the mushrooms are glossy. Serve immediately.

Spicy beanburgers

My beanburgers are nutritious, easy to make, and delicious. The kids love to prepare them and can't wait to eat them. If it's a nice day, why not slap 'em on the barbie? Make sure you squeeze as much water as possible out of the spinach; otherwise, the burgers may fall apart when they are cooked.

Preparation: 15 minutes • Cooking time: 10 minutes • Serves 2

1 tablespoon vegetable oil
1 small onion, finely chopped
2 garlic cloves
1 small red hot pepper, finely
  chopped
½ cup (100 g) frozen chopped
  spinach, thawed

15 oz (400 g) can cannellini beans
½ cup (50 g) fresh white breadcrumbs
1 teaspoon ground cumin
1 tablespoon chopped cilantro
salt and freshly ground black pepper
burger buns and salad, to serve

1 Heat the oil in a small pan and cook the onion, garlic, and hot pepper for 5 minutes until softened. Squeeze the excess moisture out of the spinach and place in a large bowl. (To get the maximum amount of water out of the spinach, place it in a dish towel and twist into a tight ball.)

2 Mash the beans well and mix with the spinach, breadcrumbs, cumin, and cilantro. Add the fried onion mixture and stir well.

3 Season to taste and with slightly wet hands, shape into 4 round burgers; pat them dry with paper towels. Grill, cook in a frying pan, or spray with oil and broil for a few minutes on each side until crisp and golden. Serve in burger buns with salad and low-fat yogurt mixed with fresh chopped herbs, if liked.

Moroccan pumpkin and potato stew

Nutrition notes
per serving:

★ calories 166
★ protein 5 g
★ carbohydrate 26 g
★ fat 5 g
★ saturated fat 1 g
★ fiber 4 g
★ added sugar none
★ salt 17.18 g

This colorful, soupy, Moroccan stew is made using harissa (a fiery paste made from dried hot peppers, garlic, salt, and olive oil). Harissa is available in tubes; look for it in specialty food stores. Serve the stew with steamed couscous to soak up all the delicious juices.

Preparation: 25 minutes • Cooking time: 40 minutes • Serves 6

2 tablespoons olive oil
1 large onion, roughly chopped
3 garlic cloves, crushed
15 oz (400 g) can chopped tomatoes
2 tablespoons harissa
1 cinnamon stick
4 cups (1 liter) vegetable stock
2 large baking potatoes, cut into
  wedges
1 lb (450 g) pumpkin or other winter
  squash, cut into wedges, peeled,
  and seeded

½ cup (150 g) baby corn
½ cup (150 g) sugar snap peas
1½ cups (300 g) cherry tomatoes
2 tablespoons cornstarch
small handful each of chopped
  fresh mint and cilantro
salt and freshly ground black pepper

1 Heat the oil in a large pan and fry the onion for 4–5 minutes over low heat until softened. Add the garlic, chopped tomatoes, harissa, cinnamon, and stock. Bring to a boil, cover, and simmer for 8–10 minutes.

2 Stir in the potatoes and bring back to the boil. Cover and simmer for 10 minutes. Stir in the pumpkin and baby corn, cover, and cook for 5 minutes more. Add the sugar snap peas and cherry tomatoes and simmer for 5 minutes, until the tomatoes just start to collapse.

3 Mix the cornstarch to a smooth paste with 4 tablespoons of water and stir into the stew. Bring to a boil, stirring until thickened. Discard the cinnamon stick and scatter over the herbs. Season to taste.

Oven-baked asparagus and tomato risotto

Oven-baking this dish is far easier than stirring the risotto over the heat for 30 minutes. I've used smoked paprika to give it a wonderful smoky flavor; the spice is available in most supermarkets. For a tasty alternative, this recipe also tastes great if you replace the asparagus with zucchini.

Preparation: 20 minutes • Cooking time: 35–40 minutes • Serves 4

2 tablespoons olive oil
1 large bunch asparagus, trimmed
½ teaspoon smoked paprika
1 onion, roughly chopped
2 garlic cloves, crushed
8 ripe plum tomatoes, roughly chopped
1 red hot pepper, seeded and finely chopped
1 teaspoon sugar
1 cup (250 g) arborio rice
2¼ cups (600 ml) boiling water
large pinch saffron strands
salt and freshly ground black pepper
fresh basil leaves, to garnish

1 Pre-heat the oven to 400°F/200°C. Heat 1 tablespoon of the oil in a large frying pan, add the asparagus and sauté for 3–4 minutes until browned. Sprinkle over the paprika. Transfer to a shallow ovenproof dish using a slotted spoon.

2 Add the remaining oil to the frying pan and fry the onion and garlic for 4–5 minutes, stirring occasionally. Add the tomatoes, hot pepper, and sugar. Season with salt and plenty of freshly ground black pepper and cook for 2 minutes. Spoon over the top of the asparagus and put the mixture on the bottom shelf of the oven.

3 Put the rice into a nonstick roasting pan, cover with the boiling water, and stir in the saffron. Cover with foil and place in the oven on the shelf above the asparagus. Cook for 20–25 minutes, until the rice is just cooked and the asparagus is tender.

4 Fluff the rice with a fork and spoon onto warmed individual serving plates. Spoon over the asparagus and tomatoes and garnish with the basil leaves.

Butternut squash and sweet potato curry

Nutrition notes per serving:

★ calories 297
★ protein 7 g
★ carbohydrate 64 g
★ fat 3 g
★ saturated fat none
★ fiber 7 g
★ added sugar none
★ salt 0.93 g

There are endless different kinds of curries, but they're usually very high in fat, so here's my tastiest-ever low-fat curry. This one is an African-inspired recipe with fruit and vegetables. I like to serve this in bowls on top of fluffy basmati rice.

Preparation: 25 minutes • Cooking time: 25–30 minutes • Serves 4

2 teaspoons vegetable oil
1 large onion, roughly chopped
3 garlic cloves, crushed
18 oz (500 g) butternut squash, seeded and cut into chunks
2 small sweet potatoes, cut into chunks
1 lb (450 g) potatoes, cut into chunks (about 2 large)
1 cooking apple, cored and cut into chunks

2 teaspoons mild curry paste or powder
1 teaspoon turmeric
1-inch (2.5-cm) piece fresh ginger, peeled and finely chopped
2 bay leaves
2 cups (500 ml) vegetable stock
4 tablespoons (50 g) raisins
salt and freshly ground black pepper
4 tablespoons low-fat plain yogurt (optional)

1 Heat the oil in a large pan and sauté the onion for 4–5 minutes until golden.

2 Add the garlic, butternut squash, sweet potatoes, potatoes, and apple. Then stir in the curry paste, turmeric, ginger, bay leaves, stock, raisins, and plenty of seasoning.

3 Bring to a boil, stir well, then cover and simmer for 15–20 minutes, stirring occasionally, until the vegetables are just tender. Spoon into bowls and add a spoonful of yogurt, if liked, or serve over basmati rice.

Hot Mexican tamale bean pie

Nutrition notes
per serving:

★ calories 317
★ protein 25 g
★ carbohydrate 36 g
★ fat 9 g
★ saturated fat 3 g
★ fiber 7 g
★ added sugar none
★ salt 1.51 g

This is just like a Mexican shepherd's pie. Use fresh hot peppers if you cannot get hold of pickled ones. To prepare the dish in advance, make up the Quorn mixture and the polenta topping separately the night before, then pop the filling into an ovenproof dish, spoon over the topping, and broil as normal.

Preparation: 20 minutes • Cooking time: 25 minutes • Serves 4

½ cup (120 g) quick-cook polenta
1 egg
scant 2 cups (450 ml) skim milk
½ cup (120 g) grated reduced-fat
  Cheddar cheese
4 tablespoons chopped cilantro
1 tablespoon vegetable oil
2 large red onions, roughly chopped
2 garlic cloves, crushed
8 pickled red hot peppers,
  roughly chopped

12 oz (350 g) pack Quorn (available
  in health-food stores)
15 oz (400 g) can chopped tomatoes
2 tablespoons tomato purée
15 oz (420 g) can mixed beans or
  black or pinto beans, drained and
  rinsed
1 cup (250 ml) vegetable stock
grated zest and juice of 1 lime
salt and freshly ground black pepper

1 Beat together the polenta, egg, milk, cheese, and 2 tablespoons of the cilantro. Season and let stand for 20 minutes to allow the polenta to swell.

2 Meanwhile, heat the oil in a large pan and fry the onions and garlic for 3–4 minutes, stirring occasionally, until softened slightly. Add 4 of the hot peppers, plus the Quorn, tomatoes, tomato purée, beans, stock, lime zest and juice, and remaining cilantro. Bring to a boil and simmer for 15 minutes. Season to taste and pour into an ovenproof dish.

3 Preheat the broiler to high. Stir the remaining hot peppers into the polenta mixture and spoon over the Quorn mixture to cover. Broil for 4–5 minutes until golden.

Smoked eggplant and vegetable curry

I use this method of smoking eggplant over a flame quite often, especially in vegetarian food. I have a friend who is vegetarian and, for health reasons, also needs to stick to a gluten-free diet. When I cook for her, I use smoked eggplant in place of flour as a thickener in sauces, soups, and stews.

Preparation: 25 minutes • Cooking time: 1 hour • Serves 6

For the spice paste
3 garlic cloves, peeled
2-inch (5-cm) piece fresh ginger, peeled and finely chopped
1 tablespoon ground cumin
1 teaspoon ground coriander
½ teaspoon ground cardamom powder
1 teaspoon ground fenugreek
1 teaspoon turmeric
2 red hot peppers, seeded
1 teaspoon salt

For the eggplant curry
1 large eggplant
13.5 oz (400 ml) can reduced-fat coconut milk
1 tablespoon vegetable oil
2 onions, cut into thin wedges
1 carrot, diagonally sliced
1 orange sweet pepper, cored, seeded, and cut into chunks
15 oz (400 g) can chopped tomatoes
15 oz (420 g) can chick peas, drained
2 large potatoes, diced
1 cup (200 g) frozen peas
fresh cilantro, to garnish

1 Work all the spice paste ingredients together in a food processor with 4 tablespoons of water to make a thick, coarse paste.

2 Pierce the eggplant with a skewer and place directly over a gas flame, or under a hot broiler: cook, turning, until charred. Transfer to a plate and let stand until cool enough to handle. Cut off the stem and halve the eggplant lengthwise. Scoop out the flesh and discard the skin. Process the flesh with the coconut milk.

3 Heat the oil in a large pan and sauté the onions for 4–5 minutes. Stir in the spice paste and fry for 2 minutes more. Add the carrot and cook for 10 minutes. Add the orange pepper, tomatoes, chick peas, potatoes,and 1¾ cups (400 ml) of water. Bring to a boil and simmer for 20 minutes. Stir in the coconut and eggplant mixture and peas. Bring to a boil and simmer for 10–15 minutes. Garnish with the cilantro and serve with basmati rice.

Pasta primavera with cherry tomato sauce

Nutrition notes
per serving:

★ calories 367
★ protein 15 g
★ carbohydrate 76 g
★ fat 3 g
★ saturated fat none
★ fiber 6 g
★ added sugar 1 g
★ salt 0.45 g

I love this no-nonsense sauce, whether it's spooned over plain pasta or simple grilled chicken. I always make mine with full-flavored vine-ripened tomatoes for the best results. However, you can use good-quality canned plum or cherry tomatoes instead for a quick, reliable sauce.

Preparation: 10 minutes • Cooking time: 15 minutes • Serves 4

1 lb (450 g) vine-ripened cherry tomatoes
pinch sugar
1 onion, finely chopped
3 garlic cloves, finely chopped
1 tablespoon fresh rosemary, finely chopped

⅔ cup (150 ml) vegetable stock
4½ cups (350 g) rigatoni
½ head broccoli, florets only
5 oz (150 g) thin green beans, trimmed
salt and freshly ground black pepper

1 Put the tomatoes, sugar, onion, garlic, rosemary, and stock into a large pan and bring to a boil. Simmer over low heat for 15 minutes, stirring occasionally, until the tomatoes have broken down and the sauce has thickened.

2 Meanwhile, cook the rigatoni in a large pan of lightly salted boiling water according to package instructions. Add the broccoli and green beans 3 minutes before the end of the cooking time.

3 Drain the rigatoni and vegetables and toss with the cherry tomato sauce. Season to taste and serve immediately.

Why not make two or three times the quantity of sauce?
You can refrigerate it or freeze it for a later date.

Salads and

Roasted onion, arugula, and
pecorino salad

Charred honey
mustard-glazed potatoes

accompaniments

Vegetable Creole-crunch salad

Light and luscious
Thai noodle salad

Spiced turkey, orange, and
watercress salad

Grilled peaches and mint
feta cheese salad

Thyme-roasted peppers and
Puy lentil salad

Pickled ginger, hot pepper,
crab, and melon salad

Grilled spiced-lime
corn on the cob

Tomato, bean, and potato
salad with gremolata

Spicy Casablanca couscous

Low-fat homemade oven fries

Roasted onion, arugula, and pecorino salad

Nutrition notes
per serving:

★ calories 77
★ protein 4 g
★ carbohydrate 5 g
★ fat 5 g
★ saturated fat 2 g
★ fiber 1 g
★ added sugar none
★ salt 0.43 g

Roasted onions are delicious, whether you use them in a soup, on a tart, or in a casserole. I like to serve them hot as a side vegetable, but they also make an extra-special salad when tossed with peppery arugula and pecorino or Parmesan cheese—and the pan juices make a lovely light dressing.

Preparation: 10 minutes • Cooking time: 30 minutes • Serves 4

12 button onions, halved
1 tablespoon olive oil
2 tablespoons balsamic vinegar
1 oz (25 g) pecorino or Parmesan

2 bunches arugula, cleaned,
  leaves only
salt and freshly ground black pepper

1 Preheat the oven to 375°F/190°C. Place the onions in a shallow roasting pan and drizzle over the oil. Season generously and drizzle over half the balsamic vinegar. Roast for 25–30 minutes, stirring halfway through, until the onions are softened and nicely browned.

2 Drizzle over the remaining balsamic vinegar and allow the onions to cool to room temperature.

3 Using a vegetable peeler, shave the pecorino or Parmesan into wafer-thin slices.

4 Arrange the arugula, roasted onions, and cheese on serving plates; drizzle with the pan juices and serve.

Charred honey mustard-glazed potatoes

Nutrition notes per serving:

★ calories 93
★ protein 2 g
★ carbohydrate 21 g
★ fat 1 g
★ saturated fat none
★ fiber 1 g
★ added sugar 3 g
★ salt 0.9 g

You can roast new potatoes from raw on your grill, but they take a while to cook through. So why not preboil them for speediness and wonderful results in this simple recipe? If you don't have a grill, you can always char them under the broiler for a similar effect.

Preparation: 10 minutes • Cooking time: 6 minutes • Serves 4

1 tablespoon Dijon mustard
1 tablespoon honey
1 tablespoon light soy sauce

8–12 new potatoes, boiled in their skins

1   Preheat the grill to high, if using. Mix together the mustard, honey, and soy sauce. Toss the potatoes in the mustard mixture and thread them onto skewers (if you use wooden ones you'll need to presoak them for 20 minutes first). Cook on the grill, or under a medium-hot broiler, for 2–3 minutes on each side until charred crisp and golden brown.

really low fat!

Vegetable Creole-crunch salad

Nutrition notes per serving:

★ calories 45
★ protein 2 g
★ carbohydrate 4 g
★ fat 2 g
★ saturated fat none
★ fiber 2 g
★ added sugar none
★ salt 0.19 g

The perfect alternative to coleslaw, with more color, more flavor—and it's healthier, too. Could the crunch get any better? Serve it up as an accompaniment to grilled meat or fish, or spoon into a fluffy baked potato—ideal for a quick healthy supper.

Preparation: 25 minutes • Cooking time: none • Serves 6

½ small head white cabbage, cored and very thinly shredded
2 celery sticks, thinly sliced
1 green pepper, cored, seeded and very thinly sliced
4 scallions, trimmed and thinly sliced
½ tablespoon Dijon mustard
1 teaspoon creamed horseradish
1 teaspoon Tabasco

1 tablespoon red wine vinegar
1 tablespoon olive oil
2 tablespoons nonfat plain yogurt
2 tablespoons chopped fresh dill (optional)
1 teaspoon caraway seeds (optional)
salt and freshly ground black pepper
pinch cayenne pepper

1 Mix the cabbage, celery, green pepper, and scallions together in a large bowl.

2 Mix the mustard, creamed horseradish, Tabasco, and vinegar in a small bowl and then gradually whisk in the oil to make a dressing. Stir in the yogurt and season well.

3 Stir the dressing, chopped dill, and caraway seeds, if using, into the vegetables just before serving so that the cabbage stays nice and crunchy. Dust all over the top with the cayenne pepper and serve.

If you have a food processor, why not use the slicing blade to cut your vegetables up evenly and quickly?

Light and luscious Thai noodle salad

Nutrition notes
per serving:

★ calories 133
★ protein 3 g
★ carbohydrate 24 g
★ fat 3 g
★ saturated fat 1 g
★ fiber none
★ added sugar none
★ salt 1.37 g

Rice noodles, or stir-fry noodles as they are sometimes called, cook in a matter of minutes. They are very light and easy to eat and soak up lots of flavor. This salad is great served as an accompaniment to any dish from the Far East.

Preparation: 10 minutes • Cooking time: 3 minutes • Serves 6

6 oz (175 g) rice vermicelli noodles
2 limes
2 small garlic cloves, very finely chopped
8 scallions, trimmed and thinly sliced
2 red hot peppers, seeded and very finely chopped

1 tablespoon peanut or sunflower oil
2 teaspoons sesame oil
3 tablespoons Thai fish sauce (nam pla)
3 tablespoons chopped cilantro

1 Drop the noodles into a large pan of boiling salted water. Take the pan off the heat and let them soak for 3 minutes.

2 Drain the noodles well, transfer them into a salad bowl, and let them cool to room temperature.

3 Finely grate the zest from 1 lime and squeeze the juice from both. Add to the noodles with the rest of the ingredients, then toss lightly together and serve.

Spiced turkey, orange, and watercress salad

Nutrition notes per serving:

★ calories 206
★ protein 33 g
★ carbohydrate 12 g
★ fat 3 g
★ saturated fat 1 g
★ fiber 2 g
★ added sugar 3 g
★ salt 0.32 g

The most intense flavor of an orange comes not from the juice, but from the essential oils in the outer layer of the skin, better known as the zest. When used along with honey and mustard as a marinade for turkey, it makes a meal that tastes truly fabulous when cooked.

Preparation: 10 minutes + marinating time • Cooking time: 5 minutes • Serves 4

finely grated zest and juice of
  1 orange
1 tablespoon honey
1 heaped teaspoon grainy Dijon
  mustard
18 oz (500 g) lean turkey breast
  strips

2 teaspoons sunflower oil
6 scallions, thinly sliced
2 bunches watercress, cleaned,
  leaves only
2 oranges, segmented
½ pint (100 g) vine-ripened cherry
  tomatoes, halved

1 Toss together the orange zest and juice, honey, mustard, and turkey strips and marinate for at least 30 minutes.

2 Heat the oil in a wok and stir-fry the turkey strips over high heat for 4–5 minutes until golden brown. Add the scallions, remove from the heat, and toss.

3 Divide the watercress, orange segments, and tomatoes between serving plates and spoon the turkey over the top. Drizzle with any pan juices and serve immediately.

Grilled peaches and mint feta cheese salad

Nutrition notes
per serving:

★ calories 198
★ protein 11 g
★ carbohydrate 14 g
★ fat 11 g
★ saturated fat 6 g
★ fiber 3 g
★ added sugar none
★ salt 1.84 g

Fruit and cheese don't have to be left until after the meal—serve them as part of your main course in this dee-lish salad. You can try using low-fat firm cheese, such as reduced-fat Cheddar, as a change from feta. Alternatively, omit the feta and serve with cottage cheese and rye crackers.

Preparation: 10 minutes • Cooking time: 3 minutes • Serves 4

1 teaspoon olive oil
4 fresh ripe peaches or nectarines, pitted and cut into wedges
finely grated zest and juice of 1 lime
4 cups (200 g) mixed salad greens
1 small red onion, halved and thinly sliced

1 cup (150 g) sugar snap peas, halved lengthwise
2 tablespoons chopped fresh mint
1 cup (200 g) feta cheese, roughly crumbled
freshly ground black pepper

1 Brush a ridged grill pan or a frying pan, with half of the oil and heat until slightly smoking. Toss the peaches or nectarines in the lime juice. Place flesh sides down onto the pan and cook for 2–3 minutes, until charred.

2 In a large bowl toss together any remaining oil and lime juice, and the lime zest, salad leaves, onion, sugar snap peas, and mint. Divide between 4 bowls or serving plates.

3 Scatter over the peaches or nectarines and the feta cheese. Season with freshly ground black pepper and serve warm.

Thyme-roasted peppers and Puy lentil salad

Nutrition notes per serving:

★ calories 228
★ protein 11 g
★ carbohydrate 33 g
★ fat 7 g
★ saturated fat 1 g
★ fiber 6 g
★ added sugar none
★ salt 0.03 g

Oven roasting most of the ingredients retains all the nutrients and really brings out the flavor of this delicious salad. It's substantial enough to serve on its own or as an accompaniment to lean grilled chicken, lamb, or fish. For vegetarians, serve with griddled halloumi cheese. Mmm!

Preparation: 20 minutes • Cooking time: 40 minutes • Serves 4

1 red sweet pepper, quartered, cored, and seeded
1 yellow or orange pepper, quartered, cored, and seeded
2 large red onions, cut into wedges
3 garlic cloves, unpeeled
leaves from 2 sprigs fresh thyme
2 tablespoons olive oil
1¼ cups (150 g) Puy lentils, rinsed
2 tablespoons balsamic vinegar
small handful of torn fresh flat-leaf parsley
salt and freshly ground black pepper

1 Preheat the oven to 400°F/200°C. Toss the peppers, onions, garlic, thyme, and oil together in a large roasting pan and roast for 35–40 minutes.

2 Meanwhile, cook the Puy lentils in a large pan of lightly salted boiling water for 20–25 minutes, until tender. Reserve 2 tablespoons of the cooking water, then drain and let cool.

3 Remove the garlic cloves from their papery skins and mash with the balsamic vinegar and reserved cooking water. Stir through the lentils with the parsley. Season to taste. Pile the roasted veggies on top to serve.

Pickled ginger, hot pepper, crab, and melon salad

Nutrition notes per serving:

* calories 114
* protein 14 g
* carbohydrate 7 g
* fat 3 g
* saturated fat 1 g
* fiber 1 g
* added sugar none
* salt 1.13 g

Pickled ginger has a wonderful affinity with fish, as anyone who's tried sushi will know. You can now buy it in most large supermarkets—it's usually found close to the sushi ingredients. I've used canned crab here for convenience, but fresh is best if you can get it.

Preparation: 10 minutes • Cooking time: none • Serves 4

2 x 7 oz (200 g) cans white
  crabmeat, drained
1 tablespoon peanut oil
1 red hot pepper, seeded and chopped
1 tablespoon roughly chopped
  pickled ginger
finely grated zest and juice of 1 lime,
  plus lime wedges, to serve

small handful of roughly chopped
  cilantro
1 red endive or small radicchio
  lettuce
1 small charentais melon or
  cantaloupe, seeded, peeled,
  and sliced
salt and freshly ground black pepper

1 In a large bowl, toss the crabmeat, oil, hot pepper, pickled ginger, lime zest and juice, and cilantro together and season to taste.

2 Arrange 3 or 4 leaves of red endive on each serving plate, place the slices of melon between the leaves, and pile the crabmeat in the center. Garnish with a sprig of cilantro and serve with lime wedges to squeeze over.

Grilled spiced-lime corn on the cob

There really is nothing like freshly grilled corn on the cob. Some people like to peel off the husks (the green papery leaves surrounding the corn), but I think they act as natural protection and prevent the kernels from becoming dry and hard instead of tender and juicy like these.

Preparation: 5 minutes • Cooking time: 10 minutes • Serves 4

4 ears of corn
2 limes, each cut into 4 wedges

1 teaspoon salt
½ teaspoon cayenne pepper

1 Pull the husks back from the corn, then remove and discard the silk (the fine feathery strands inside the husks). Rub each ear with a wedge of lime, then fold back the husks to cover the kernels.

2 Cook over medium-hot coals for about 10 minutes, turning frequently, until the corn is dark golden and the kernels tender.

3 Mix together the salt and cayenne pepper.

4 Pull the husks back away from the corn and sprinkle over the salt mixture. Serve with a wedge of lime for extra rubbing.

Tomato, bean, and potato salad with gremolata

Nutrition notes
per serving:

★ calories 171
★ protein 7 g
★ carbohydrate 29 g
★ fat 4 g
★ saturated fat 1 g
★ fiber 6 g
★ added sugar none
★ salt 0.32 g

Simple to make, stunning to look at, and great to eat—what more could you want? Gremolata is an aromatic mixture of zesty lemon, pungent garlic, and flavorful flat-leaf parsley. Serve this salad warm or cold, with plenty of crusty bread to mop up all those tasty juices.

Preparation: 15 minutes • Cooking time: 15 minutes • Serves 4

8–12 small new potatoes, scrubbed, cut into bite-sized pieces if necessary
8 oz (225 g) runner or green beans, cut diagonally into slices
6 ripe mixed tomatoes (e.g., plum tomatoes, quartered lengthwise; yellow and red cherry tomatoes, halved; beefsteak tomatoes, cut into wedges)

4 scallions, thinly sliced
8 oz (200 g) young spinach leaves
2 ripe tomatoes, peeled and seeded
1 tablespoon pesto
salt and freshly ground black pepper
For the gremolata
1 small lemon
2 garlic cloves, finely chopped
handful of flat-leaf parsley, roughly torn

1 Cook the potatoes in a large pan of lightly salted boiling water for 10–12 minutes or until just tender. Add the runner beans and cook for 2 minutes more. Then drain and rinse under cold running water.

2 Toss the potatoes and beans with the mixed tomatoes, scallions, and spinach, and season to taste.

3 For the gremolata, use a vegetable peeler to pare thin strips of rind from the lemon. Carefully remove as much white pith as possible (this is bitter). Finely chop the yellow lemon zest and toss with the garlic and parsley. Season and set aside. Squeeze the juice from the lemon and work in a food processor with the peeled tomatoes and pesto for 10–15 seconds. Pour over the potato mixture and toss through. Scatter over the gremolata to serve.

Spicy Casablanca couscous

A wonderfully zestful combination of couscous, fresh herbs, spices, and pine nuts—delicious served with roasted vegetables as a vegetarian main course and a fabulous accompaniment to any grilled fish or meat. Why not make it for a picnic lunch, or take it to work for a lunchtime snack?

Nutrition notes
per serving:

★ calories 117
★ protein 3 g
★ carbohydrate 13 g
★ fat 6 g
★ saturated fat 1 g
★ fiber none
★ added sugar none
★ salt 0.13 g

Preparation: 10 minutes • Cooking time: 5 minutes + standing time • Serves 10

2 tablespoons olive oil
1 garlic clove, very finely chopped
1 tablespoon ground cumin
1 teaspoon ground coriander
1 teaspoon paprika
1½ cups (350 ml) chicken or
  vegetable stock
good pinch saffron strands

6 scallions, trimmed and thinly sliced
1 cup (225 g) couscous
coarsely grated zest and juice of
  1 lemon
2 red hot peppers, seeded and very
  finely chopped
4 tablespoons (50 g) pine nuts,
  toasted

1 Heat 1 tablespoon of the oil in a large pan. Add the garlic, cumin, coriander, and paprika and sauté over gentle heat for 1 minute, stirring.

2 Add the stock and saffron and bring to a boil. Add the scallions, then pour in the couscous in a steady stream and give it a quick stir.

3 Cover the pan with a tight-fitting lid, remove from the heat, and set aside for 5 minutes, to allow the grains to swell and absorb the stock.

4 If you are serving this warm, stir in the rest of the oil and the remaining ingredients now. Otherwise, let the couscous cool, then chill in the refrigerator for 1 hour before adding all the other ingredients for a deliciously cold couscous salad.

Low-fat homemade oven fries

Nutrition notes
per serving:

★ calories 190
★ protein 5 g
★ carbohydrate 31 g
★ fat 6 g
★ saturated fat 1 g
★ fiber 2 g
★ added sugar none
★ salt 0.85 g

Normal deep-fried potatoes contain 350 calories per portion, but these low-fat ones contain only 80. They're still quite high in calories . . . but we all need a treat now and then! Russet potatoes, often called Idaho potatoes in grocery stores, make the best fries.

Preparation: 15 minutes • Cooking time: 20 minutes • Serves 4

1½ lbs (700 g) potatoes
4 cups (1 liter) boiling stock
  (meat or vegetable)

2 tablespoons vegetable oil
paprika to taste

1 Preheat the oven to 425°F/220°C.

2 Cut the potatoes into thick sticks. Plunge into a pan containing the boiling stock and cook for up to 5 minutes, until just tender.

3 Drain in a colander (reserving the stock for another batch of chips or to use in a soup or sauce). Let cool slightly.

4 Put the oil in a large freezer bag or plastic food container and carefully toss the potatoes in the fat. (At this point you can freeze them for later use, once they are cold.)

5 Transfer the fries to a lightly greased or nonstick baking sheet and bake for 10–15 minutes, turning them once or twice, until golden and crisp. If cooking from frozen, allow 15–20 minutes. Sprinkle with paprika rather than salt, and serve.

Not-so-

naughty desserts

Star-anise-scented
strawberries

Golden apricot and raisin
rice pudding

Iced passion-fruit platter

Trim tiramisu

Hot-grilled peaches with
pistachio brittle

Live-and-kicking lemon and
hot-pepper sorbet

Deep-pan rhubarb soufflé

Iced caffe latte cups

Fruity coconut yogurt treat

Energy-booster smoothies:
Mango and banana smoothie
Sweet berry smoothie
Watermelon smoothie

Fresh cherryade

Star-anise-scented strawberries

Nutrition notes per serving:

★ calories 126
★ protein 2 g
★ carbohydrate 30 g
★ fat 1 g
★ saturated fat none
★ fiber 1 g
★ added sugar 16 g
★ salt 0.02 g

The Chinese spice star anise is now widely available. It tastes like licorice and adds a lovely spicy flavor to your cooking. It is the perfect ingredient to give fruit a real lift, especially strawberries. Serve the strawberries on their own or spooned over low-fat ice cream, sorbet, or crispy meringues.

Preparation: 5 minutes • Cooking time: 7 minutes + chilling time • Serves 2

½ pint (225 g) small fresh
 strawberries
⅔ cup (150 ml) fresh orange juice
2 tablespoons sugar

1 star anise
1 teaspoon caraway seeds
meringues and low-fat plain yogurt,
 to serve

1 Hull the strawberries, place them in a bowl, and set aside.

2 Place the orange juice, sugar, star anise, and caraway seeds in a small pan. Bring to a boil and simmer for 5 minutes, then pour over the strawberries and allow to cool. Chill for at least an hour and up to 8 hours.

3 Divide the strawberries between 2 glasses and serve accompanied by meringues and a spoonful of low-fat yogurt.

Golden apricot and raisin rice pudding

really low fat!

Nutrition notes
per serving:

★ calories 373
★ protein 9 g
★ carbohydrate 82 g
★ fat 3 g
★ saturated fat 2 g
★ fiber 2 g
★ added sugar 41 g
★ salt 0.27 g

This is a great standby dessert using only eight ingredients, most of which you may well have in your cupboard. Flaked rice makes this dessert incredibly quick; buy it at a specialty food store or subsitute medium-grain rice. You can serve the pudding either hot or cold, whichever suits you best.

Preparation: 10 minutes • Cooking time: 20 minutes • Serves 4

12 dried apricots
2 tablespoons (50 g) golden raisins
1 lemon
⅓ cup (75 g) flaked or medium-
   grain rice

3 cups (750 ml) milk
4 tablespoons (50 g) sugar
8 tablespoons apricot jam
fresh mint sprigs, to decorate

1 Reserve 4 of the dried apricots, then chop the rest. Mix with the golden raisins and set aside. Using a vegetable peeler, cut wide strips of rind from the lemon.

2 Place the lemon-rind strips, rice, milk, and sugar in a pan and bring to a boil, then reduce the heat and simmer for 12–15 minutes, stirring often. Stir in the dried fruit, divide between serving bowls, and set aside to cool slightly.

3 To make the apricot glaze, squeeze 1 tablespoon of juice from the lemon into a small pan. Stir in 2 tablespoons of water, then add the jam. Bring to a boil, stirring, until the jam has melted, then immediately remove from the heat. Let cool for a few minutes until slightly thickened, then pour over the rice puddings. Decorate each with a dried apricot and a mint sprig.

Iced passion-fruit platter

This beautiful fruit platter is a great finish to a dinner party as it looks stunning and is simple to prepare. It is also a very good palate cleanser after a tasty meal. I've served it here with a fruity passion-fruit cream—yes, it does contain real cream—and it's still low in fat!

Preparation: 20 minutes • Cooking time: none • Serves 8

1 papaya
1 mango
1 small pineapple
4 kiwi fruit
1 small galia, charentais, cantaloupe, or honeydew melon

For the passion-fruit cream
4 passion fruits
⅔ cup (150 ml) light cream
finely grated zest of ½ small orange
2 tablespoons confectioners' sugar
2 tablespoons fresh orange juice
5 tablespoons nonfat plain yogurt

1 For the passion-fruit cream, cut the passion fruit in half and scoop out the pulp into a bowl.

2 Whip the cream, orange zest, and confectioners' sugar into soft peaks and then gradually whisk in the orange juice, yogurt, and passion-fruit pulp so that the mixture remains softly whipped. Spoon the mixture into a small serving bowl, cover, and chill in the refrigerator.

3 Cut the fruits into bite-sized pieces. Place on a tray and cover. Put in the refrigerator until just before you are ready to serve.

4 Arrange the chilled prepared fruits attractively on a large ice-filled serving platter around the bowl of passion-fruit cream.

Trim tiramisu

Nutrition notes
per serving:

★ calories 389
★ protein 22 g
★ carbohydrate 64 g
★ fat 5 g
★ saturated fat 2 g
★ fiber 1 g
★ added sugar 47 g
★ salt 0.26 g

We all love to indulge in a wicked dessert now and then, and tiramisu is always a favorite. With my version you really can indulge. What's more, it's so delicious that you won't even notice that you've chosen the healthy option.

Preparation: 20 minutes • Cooking time: none • Serves 4

6 tablespoons (75 g) sugar
2 x 8 oz (250 g) tubs Quark (lowfat
  soft cheese, available in health-
  food stores))
5 tablespoons skim milk
1 large vanilla pod, split and seeds
  scraped out

3 tablespoons Kahlúa (coffee liqueur)
4 tablespoons strong black coffee
8 ladyfingers, snapped in half
½ pint (100 g) mixed blueberries and
  raspberries
2 oz (50 g) dark chocolate,
  finely grated

1 In a large bowl beat together the sugar, Quark, milk, and vanilla seeds until smooth.

2 Mix the coffee liqueur and coffee together in a large bowl. Dip 4 ladyfingers into the coffee mixture and arrange in the bottom of individual dessert glasses. Scatter over half the blueberries and raspberries and spoon over half the creamy vanilla mixture. Sprinkle over half the grated chocolate.

3 Repeat all over again to use up all the ingredients—starting with the ladyfingers and finishing with a sprinkling of grated chocolate. Chill for at least 30 minutes before serving.

Hot grilled peaches with pistachio brittle

Nutrition notes per serving:

★ calories 268
★ protein 7 g
★ carbohydrate 51 g
★ fat 3 g
★ saturated fat none
★ fiber 2 g
★ added sugar 38 g
★ salt 0.1 g

I love this dessert because of all the different textures you get in one mouthful! Sweet, sticky peaches with cool, creamy yogurt and crisp, nutty brittle . . . who needs all that whipped cream? This fruit-and-nut dessert tastes absolutely great without it.

Preparation: 10 minutes • Cooking time: 15–20 minutes • Serves 4

½ cup (100 g) sugar
2 tablespoons (25 g) shelled pistachio nuts, roughly chopped
4 ripe peaches, halved and pitted
4 tablespoons port

2 tablespoons red jelly (i.e., strawberry, cherry, redcurrant)
8 oz (200 g) carton nonfat plain yogurt

1 Preheat the grill to high. Line a baking pan with a silicon liner (see tip, opposite). Sprinkle two-thirds of the sugar into the bottom of a heavy-based pan, sprinkle over the pistacho nuts, and heat gently until the sugar has dissolved. Increase the heat and cook for 2–3 minutes more, until the mixture is a golden color. Immediately pour the mixture onto the lined baking tray and leave to cool and harden. (It's essential that you do this quickly as the sugar turns from golden to black in seconds.)

2 Meanwhile, put the peaches, cut sides up, into an ovenproof dish. Warm the port and redcurrant jelly together in a small pan until runny. Pour over the peaches. Sprinkle the remaining sugar over the peaches and broil for 8–10 minutes until sticky and golden.

3 Spoon the peaches and sauce onto individual serving plates. Spoon a dollop of yogurt at the side. Roughly break up the pistachio brittle and scatter over the top.

I always use silicon liners, which are available from most good cooking stores. They are black baking liners made from silicon components. They're great as you can wash and use them again and again—and they're *really* nonstick!

Live-and-kicking lemon and hot-pepper sorbet

The cool lemon sorbet complements the sweet kick of the glazed hot peppers. You can make the sorbet up to 4 months in advance—simply freeze it and move it into the fridge 15 minutes before you want to serve it. I like to serve the sorbet with a splash of vodka for a special occasion. Woweee!

Preparation: 15 minutes + freezing time • Cooking time: 10 minutes
• Serves 6

½ cup (100 g) sugar
2 red hot peppers, seeded, halved,
  and thinly sliced
finely grated zest and juice of
  4 lemons

3 tablespoons honey
1 large egg white
6 tablespoons vodka

1 Sprinkle all but 2 tablespoons of the sugar into a large pan. Add 2¼ cups (600 ml) of cold water and the hot peppers. Heat gently, stirring occasionally, until the sugar has dissolved. Bring to a boil and boil rapidly for 5 minutes. Remove the hot peppers with a slotted spoon and coat in the remaining sugar. Spread the sugared hot peppers, spaced well apart, on a sheet of waxed paper and let dry for about 20 minutes.

2 Add the lemon zest and juice and honey to the sugar syrup and let cool completely. Pour into a freezerproof container, seal, and freeze for 3–4 hours until slushy.

3 Break up the sorbet with a fork and spoon into a large bowl. Beat with a fork until smooth. Whisk the egg white until stiff and fold into the lemon sorbet mixture. Pour back into the container and freeze until solid or ready to use.

4 Scoop the sorbet into glasses, sprinkling each scoop with some of the glazed hot peppers. Pour over the vodka and top with a pile of the remaining hot peppers.

Deep-pan rhubarb soufflé

Nutrition notes
per serving:

★ calories 170
★ protein 5.5 g
★ carbohydrate 24.6 g
★ fat 6.2 g
★ saturated fat 2.44 g
★ fiber 1.2 g
★ added sugar 22.3 g
★ salt 0.19 g

This wonderfully light soufflé omelette is packed full of juicy, spiced rhubarb and strawberries and is on the table in less than 20 minutes. As an alternative filling I like to use banana, mango, and brown sugar, or pineapple pieces and preserved ginger.

Preparation: 10 minutes • Cooking time: 10 minutes • Serves 4

3 stalks rhubarb, cut into
  1-inch (2.5-cm) pieces, or 9 oz
  (250 g) frozen rhubarb pieces
1 tablespoon orange juice or water
4 tablespoons sugar
good pinch mixed spice
½ pint (100 g) strawberries, sliced

3 eggs, separated
1 teaspoon finely grated orange zest
1 tablespoon butter
confectioners' sugar, for dusting
4 tablespoons reduced-fat crème
  fraîche or reduced-fat sour cream,
  to serve

1 Place the rhubarb, orange juice or water, 3 tablespoons of the sugar, and the mixed spice in a pan and bring to a boil; simmer for 4 minutes until tender and thickened. Stir in the strawberries and set aside.

2 Beat the egg yolks and remaining sugar until pale, then stir in the orange zest. In a separate bowl, whisk the egg whites until stiff. Fold the egg yolks carefully into the whites.

3 Preheat the broiler to medium. Melt the butter in a 9-inch (23-cm) frying pan and spoon in the egg mixture so it covers the bottom. Cook over gentle heat for a few minutes until golden underneath and beginning to set, then broil for 1 minute until golden and puffy.

4 Slide the soufflé onto a serving plate and spoon some of the fruit and sauce over half of it. Fold over and dust liberally with confectioners' sugar. Serve in wedges with extra fruit and a spoonful of crème fraîche.

Iced caffe latte cups

Nutrition notes
per serving:

★ calories 202
★ protein 8 g
★ carbohydrate 22 g
★ fat 10 g
★ saturated fat 6 g
★ fiber none
★ added sugar 11 g
★ salt 0.34 g

This is my favorite hot drink turned into a dreamy ice cream. You can prepare these cups ahead of schedule, but remember to transfer the frozen treats to the refrigerator one hour before serving. This ensures they will be at just the right soft-set when you come to eat them. Yum!

Preparation: 5 minutes + freezing time • Cooking time: none • Serves 6

4 tablespoons golden sugar
1/2 cup (100 ml) freshly made
  espresso coffee
15 oz (420 ml) can reduced-fat
  evaporated milk

1¼ cups (300 ml) light cream or
  half and half
handful of roasted coffee beans

1 Stir the sugar into the coffee until dissolved. Mix in the evaporated milk and cream.

2 Pour into coffee cups and scatter 4 or 5 coffee beans on top of each. Freeze for several hours until frozen solid. About 1 hour before serving, transfer to the refrigerator.

Fruity coconut yogurt treat

Preparation: 15 minutes • Cooking time: none • Serves 4

¾ pint (350 g) strawberries, halved or sliced

2 nectarines or peaches, pitted and sliced

½ pint (100 g) blueberries or black grapes

1 large banana

½ cup (120 ml) fresh orange juice

8 oz (200 g) carton nonfat plain yogurt

2 tablespoons dried coconut, toasted

1 Mix together the strawberries, nectarines or peaches, and blueberries or grapes and divide between tall sundae glasses.

2 To make the fruit smoothie, roughly chop the banana, then place in a food processor or blender with the orange juice and yogurt and work until smooth.

3 Pour the smoothie over the fruit in the bowls and sprinkle each with toasted dried coconut.

Energy-booster smoothies

A smoothie is a delicious summer drink. Blends of fruit, yogurt, milk, and juice, they're packed full of goodness and perfect for a super boost first thing in the morning. Choose your favorite fruit and vegetables and mix and match to get the flavors you really like. Here are a few of my ideas to get you started.

Mango and banana smoothie

Preparation: 5 minutes • Cooking time: none • Serves 2

Nutrition notes
per serving:

★ calories 296
★ protein 9 g
★ carbohydrate 64 g
★ fat 2 g
★ saturated fat 1 g
★ fiber 6 g
★ added sugar none
★ salt 0.23 g

1 large ripe mango
1 large banana, roughly chopped
1 cup (240 ml) 1% milk
1 cup (240 ml) fresh orange
  juice

3 tablespoons nonfat plain
  yogurt
crushed ice, to serve

1 Peel the mango and discard the pit. Roughly chop the flesh and put into a blender or food processor with the remaining ingredients; work until smooth and thick. Pour over crushed ice and drink immediately.

Sweet berry smoothie

Preparation: 5 minutes • Cooking time: none • Serves 2

Nutrition notes
per serving:

★ calories 123
★ protein 5 g
★ carbohydrate 24 g
★ fat 1 g
★ saturated fat none
★ fiber 2 g
★ added sugar 6 g
★ salt 0.18 g

½ pint (225 g) mixed strawberries,
  raspberries, and blueberries
2 kiwi fruit, peeled and roughly
  chopped

6 oz (150 g) carton low-fat
  plain yogurt
1 tablespoon honey
ice cubes, to serve

1 Put all the ingredients into a blender or food processor and blend for 1 minute until smooth. Pour over ice cubes and drink immediately.

For a really cool mango and banana smoothie, peel the banana, wrap in plastic wrap, and place in the freezer for 1–2 hours. Remove the wrap, cut the banana in half, and finish off the smoothie as normal.

Nutrition notes
per serving:

★ calories 174
★ protein 6 g
★ carbohydrate 35 g
★ fat 2 g
★ saturated fat none
★ fiber 1 g
★ added sugar none
★ salt 0.16 g

Watermelon smoothie

Don't worry too much about the actual amount of the melon; just use more or less yogurt to suit your fancy.

Preparation: 10 minutes • Cooking time: none • Serves 2

½ small watermelon, about
  3¼ lb (1.5 kg), peeled, seeded,
  and cubed

8 ice cubes
6 oz (150 g) carton low-fat
  plain yogurt

1 Pass the watermelon through a juicer.

2 Place the ice cubes in a glass pitcher and mix with the yogurt; pour in the watermelon juice, mixing well. Pour into glasses and drink the smoothie immediately.

Nutrition notes
per serving:

★ calories 91
★ protein 0.8 g
★ carbohydrate 23.4 g
★ fat 0.1 g
★ saturated fat none
★ fiber 0.8 g
★ added sugar 13.1 g
★ salt 0.02 g

Fresh cherryade

This is a fragrant drink that's really refreshing and fantastic for picnics and barbecues. Just you watch it disappear!

Preparation: 10 minutes + cooling time • Cooking time: 10 minutes
• Serves 4

1 lb (450 g) fresh cherries,
  plus extra for garnish
4 tablespoons (50 g) sugar
1 sprig fresh tarragon

juice of 2 limes
2¼ cups (600 ml) soda water
ice and lime twists, to serve

1 Place the cherries, sugar, and tarragon in a small pan with 2 cups (450 ml) of water. Gently bring to a boil, stirring until the sugar dissolves, then simmer for 10 minutes until the cherries are very soft.

2 Remove from the heat, then press through a sieve to remove the pits and tarragon and purée the cherries. Stir in the lime juice, then chill until ready to serve.

3 Transfer to a pitcher and top off with soda water. Pour into ice-filled glasses and serve garnished with lime twists and fresh cherries.

I use a juicer for making smoothies, but if you don't
have one you can use a blender instead.

Index

Page numbers in **bold** indicate recipes. Page numbers in *italics* refer to illustrations.